KT-116-482

coolcamping
scotland

Keith Didcock, Andy Stothert,
Robin McKelvie and Jenny McKelvie

The publishers assert their right to use
Cool Camping as a trademark of Punk Publishing Ltd.

Cool Camping: Scotland (2nd edition)
First edition published in 2007
This second edition published in the United Kingdom in 2010 by
Punk Publishing Ltd
3 The Yard
Pegasus Place
London
SE11 5SD

www.punkpublishing.co.uk
www.coolcamping.co.uk

A catalogue record of this book is available from the British Library.

ISBN: 978-1-906889-04-3 2nd edition
(ISBN 978-0-9552036-33 1st edition)

10 9 8 7 6 5 4 3

introduction

Scotland is, of course, a land of some renown. With its Celtic culture, hardy people and eccentric cuisine, it's a land rich in intrigue. With its tartan, whisky and ginger hair, it's a land rich in cliché. With its cast of doomed heroes like Mary Queen of Scots, Bonnie Prince Charlie and the 1978 World Cup football team, it's a land rich in pathos. And with its spectacular and diverse scenery, it's a land rich in beauty. But unlike the heavily mapped and tramped terrain of England and Wales, it's still terra incognita for many people.

Hopefully this second edition of *Cool Camping: Scotland* will change all that and open your eyes to the wonders that await the intrepid camper north of the border. Once again we have criss-crossed the land to seek out the finest camping this country has to offer. We've been up glen and over moor, round Highland and island, over sea loch and burn and even stopped off in Edinburgh to catch our breath and take in a festival show.

We've revisited old friends, made loads of new ones and sadly had to say goodbye to an old favourite – Achnahaird Farm in Achiltibuie on the wild Atlantic coast was *numero uno* in the Top 5 in our first edition in 2007, but has unfortunately since closed

down. That's the bad news. The good news is that there are rumours a new site will open across the hills at Altandhu, so keep your eyes peeled and fingers crossed.

The other good news is that we've added 20 great new sites to this edition and found an exciting variety of different places. Unlike in England and Wales, luxury camping has never been a big thing in Scotland. Whereas down south the fields abound with yurts full of sequined cushions, easy-sleep futons and wood-burning stoves, up in Scotland it's always been a little more austere. But nowadays that old hard-nosed Calvinist spirit, which says that if you enjoy yourself today you'll pay for it tomorrow, is slowly giving way to a more accommodating attitude to personal comfort and enjoyment. And sites like Comrie Croft (p63) in Perthshire are paving the way.

Given the sparse population in thousands of square miles of wilderness, it's no surprise that we've found a few more gloriously remote little boltholes, like the charming Camus More (p179) on the northern tip of Skye. But for those who like the bright lights and the big city, there are new entries near Edinburgh, like Blinkbonny Wood (p37) or just across the Forth Road Bridge in Fife, like Woodland Camping Gimme Shelter (p45). We've added a few more sites on the western isles, too, like Kintra Farm (p17) on Islay and the magnificent Lickisto Blackhouse (p183) among the lunar landscape of Harris.

For this edition we've also added in a couple of features to help you make the most of your time in Scotland. There's a section on great walks and wheel trails (p86) around the country if you fancy stepping out to stretch your legs or go for a spin. And taking account of the chance that at some point during your trip you're likely to have to shelter from the Scottish weather, we've also picked out our favourite festivals for you (see p236), from the glorious St Magnus Festival in Orkney to the grittier but funnier Glasgow International Comedy Festival.

We've also got a thing or two to say about wild camping (see p160), which was a prospect we embraced with enthusiasm in the first edition of *Cool Camping: Scotland* in 2007. Now we're a little more ambivalent, as the downside to allowing all and sundry to set up for the night wherever they like has started to cause a few problems. It's still a glorious opportunity to enjoy unfettered access to the country, but with rights come responsibilities and we would urge everyone who likes it wild to treat the countryside with respect by following just a few simple dos and don'ts.

Whether your thing is creature comfort or wild and free, we're sure there are sites here to tickle your fancy. There's not much we can do about the twin curses of the Scottish summer – midges and rain – but our extensive experiments with insect repellent and wet-weather gear have provided scientific proof that human beings can prosper in the Scottish climate. As they say, there's no such thing as bad weather – only inappropriate clothing.

So don your mac and slap on some anti-midge cream. Tuck a copy of *Cool Camping: Scotland* and a caramel wafer under your arm and, with one cavalier swig from a can of Irn-Bru, be bold and go forth into the big blue Scottish yonder. It's all out there just waiting to be discovered.

campsite locator

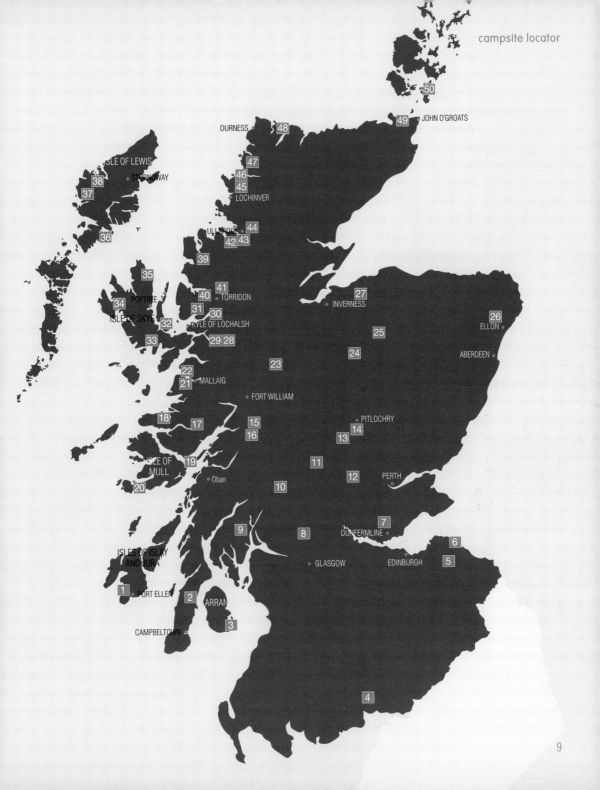

JOHN O'GROATS

DURNESS

ISLE OF LEWIS

STORNOWAY

LOCHINVER

ULLAPOOL

INVERNESS

ELLON

PORTREE

TORRIDON

ISLE OF SKYE

KYLE OF LOCHALSH

ABERDEEN

MALLAIG

FORT WILLIAM

PITLOCHRY

ISLE OF MULL

Oban

PERTH

DUNFERMLINE

EDINBURGH

GLASGOW

ISLES OF ISLAY AND JURA

PORT ELLEN

ARRAN

CAMPBELTOWN

9

1   2

3   4

cool camping top 5

Of course it's difficult. How do you choose between juicy apples and plump pears?
The answer is to make a fruit salad. Here are the six ingredients you need for
a fruitful Scottish camping trip. Just add cream and enjoy.

It's straight in at Number One for Harvey and John's eccentric little oasis in the barren
moonscape of the Isle of Harris. Everything a quirky campsite should be.

Feel the force of the Atlantic, as well as the atmosphere, at Ardnamurchan, the westernmost
campsite in mainland Britain. Hand-cut terraces with views across the water give the place
a vibe that defies rational description.

The top-ranked survivor from the first edition, this place is an advert for eco-sustainability
with its dapple of islands, stunning beaches, grass-covered dunes and azure waters.

Seven miles down a single-track road, with its own bay and in the shadow of the Skye
mountains, Glenbrittle remains a special little place to savour.

Magical Lazy Duck's the perfect tiny campsite with a back-garden feel. With its hammocks
between the pine trees, sauna, the ducks and the birds, it's a blissful place to chill.

The very model of a modish modern campsite, Comrie Croft has camping down to a T with a
wild wood, Swedish kåtas and a small lake to boot.

campsites at a glance

ON YER BIKE

Most of the sites listed have decent cycling in the near vicinity.

kintra farm

Scotland's famous for quite a few things. Some, like Scottish goalkeeping and the penchant for deep-fried confectionery, are bad. Some, like the Bay City Rollers and the 1978 World Cup campaign, are best brushed under the carpet. And some, like Sean Connery and Kenny Dalgleish, are good. But nothing epitomises Scotland quite so much as its whisky. It's the national tipple, the country's major export and the nectar that wets the pens of its bards. And perhaps nowhere is the Scottish whisky industry on better display than the Isle of Islay. Don't tell Speyside (Scotland's other major whisky region) but Islay has a good claim to being Scotland's whisky capital, as this wee island boasts many of the finest, darkest, peatiest malts around from the south of the island as well as some less pungent spring-water malts from the north.

Just a short ferry hop from the Mull of Kintyre, Islay is relatively accessible without a full expedition party and a six-week supply of Kendal Mint Cake, so there's no excuse not to pop over and take a look for yourself.

The island was once the seat of the mighty 'Lords of the Isles'; the MacDonald clan and Lord Islay virtually ran Scotland in the 18th century after the Act of Union – when England, Wales and Scotland officially became the Kingdom of Great Britain. It seems odd that such a small island should be such a powerful force in Scotland. After all, there's not much here apart from birdlife and whisky distilleries. But then, wait a minute…Perhaps it was the whisky that put all that fire in the bellies of the island's inhabitants. Long before the days of Irn-Bru, maybe it was whisky that had this little island thinking it ruled the land.

The ferry berths in the tranquil little town of Port Ellen, a planned village built and named in the 19th century. A curve of bay and some old-style four-square houses facing the water make the place an ideal spot for a wander and a reflective hour or two on one of the benches on the green (if the weather's clement, that is). Compared with the majority of the rest of the island, the town is a bustling hive of activity with a Co-op, a cyber café and a couple of pubs, and it's on the road towards the three southern distilleries.

Heading out of town in the other direction you are quickly into the open country of rolling hills and moorland that give the southern malts (Laphroaig, Lagavulin and Ardbeg) their distinctive strong and peaty flavour. It's the rain that falls here that filters through the peat that feeds the streams that end up on the rocks in that glass in your hand.

Across all that moorland and farmland you'll find the site at Kintra. It's a working farm that just happens to have great beach frontage fringed with grassy dunes. You can shelter down in one of the dips or pitch the tent (make it a strong, three-season one) up high if you want that real wind-in-your-hair, salt-on-the-skin feel. The bonus for the brave is the view of the stretching sands of the Traigh Mhòr sweeping off to the north with the bare hills behind and the Rhinns of Islay across the choppy waters of Laggan Bay.

Out on the water are all kinds of possibilities for boogie board and sail, surfboard and kite and so on. Or you could just enjoy a swim. Whatever you do, it's only a short scramble back into the marram grass and dunes to your tent or camper for a warming dram of one of the local tipples.

THE UPSIDE Beachside camping on the wonderful Isle of Islay.

THE DOWNSIDE It can be a hike from your pitch to the facilities.

THE DAMAGE £3 per adult and £1.50 per child (aged 5–14) plus £4–10 per tent and £6–10 for campers/motorhomes (both depending on size). No charge for dogs, but please keep them on their leads.

THE FACILITIES Back at the farmhouse you'll find 2 showers and 2 lavatories for guys and girls. There are also dishwashing facilities, a washing machine and a modest seating area to keep out of whatever the weather has in store. Note that there are no electric hook-ups on the site.

NEAREST DECENT PUB You have to go back to Port Ellen to the White Hart (01496 300120; on the left as you reach the town). It won't win too many awards, but the alternative is the dingy little Ardview Inn on the waterfront.

IF IT RAINS Well, there are 8 whisky distilleries on Islay, some of which produce the finest malts in Scotland, so it would make sense to take a tour. Choose whichever one best suits your tastebuds, but it's advisable to book ahead. Tours details can be found in pdf form at www.blog.islayinfo.com.

GETTING THERE From the ferry at Port Ellen turn left for Bowmore and just before the large malting factory turn left at the sign for Mull of Oa. Follow this road until the signpost for Kintra (dead ahead) and the road takes you all the way to the farmhouse.

OPEN Apr–late Sept.

IF IT'S FULL There's a site at the Port Mòr Centre, Port Charlotte (01496 850441). Otherwise it's a case of wild camping (see p160 for tips).

Kintra Farm, Port Ellen, Isle of Islay PA42 7AT

| t | 01496 302051 | w | www.kintrafarm.co.uk | 1 | on the map |

muasdale

Fancy a challenge? How about heading down a seeming road to nowhere in search of Kintyre, a place that truly encapsulates the phrase 'out on a limb'?

The various sea lochs that bite so deeply into Scotland's western fringe make getting anywhere near Kintyre a long and arduous undertaking, involving a route around the shores of both Loch Lomond and Loch Fyne. A scenic detour, it's a trip of some 150 miles from Glasgow – all to end up at a point just 60 miles south of where it began. Small wonder, then, that few folk wander this way, leaving Kintyre relatively unmolested. There is a slightly less circuitous way of reaching these inaccessible acres, and that's by crossing the two lochs aboard a ferry. It may not be any quicker, but it is more relaxed and even feels a little exotic.

But is Kintyre really worth all that travel time? After all, there are no desperately challenging mountains to look at (or scale for that matter), neither is there anywhere of fame or notoriety around. Except, of course, for the Mull of Kintyre, where you might just come across Sir Paul McCartney brandishing a set of bagpipes.

Well, rest assured that the doubts that may have plagued you along the way, despite all the glorious scenes en route, are bound to evaporate from even the grumpiest of souls on reaching this very special place. Perching on not-so-towering cliffs that measure just over a metre in height, Muasdale Holiday Park sits directly above the purest white sands. The calm waters that reside in this bay are so sheltered that, despite the campsite's proximity to the water's edge, there's no danger of sharing your sleeping bag with the sea.

The beach itself is exceedingly beautiful and the water is (we're assured) warm enough for extended bathing – as opposed to the dip 'n' scream session you'd normally steel yourself for – but what really stole the hearts and minds of the *Cool Camping* rabble was the view over the water to the islands of Islay and Jura. It wouldn't be out of the question to simply sit here with a good book for a whole week, occasionally glancing around to confirm you've won big in the lottery of life.

The campsite – part of the tiny straggling village of Muasdale, which has retained an air of genuine everyday life about it as tourism is yet to trouble these parts – takes up a slither of well-drained, midge-free ground between a main road and the sea; and with no more than 15 pitches available, it's rather small. The official *Cool Camping*

inspection took place over the school holidays, but the place wasn't full, nor did the road prove noisy at night, even though we slept right next to it.

Should you finish your book, hole your canoe, break your bucket and spade or lose your Speedos, it's worth popping your derrière on to a bike saddle, as the mainly flat road on the western side of Kintyre is made for two wheelers. The ferry to the small island of Gigha is a four-mile pedal; or, to present your thighs with a real challenge, cycle the amazingly scenic road on the eastern side of the peninsula. Surf dudes and chicks can find some serious waves at Machrihanish Bay. Another great day out can be had at a distillery tour on Islay, where some of the finest malts in the world are produced (see p17). If you do take your bike over, stick to the east of the island and enjoy the wildly impressive sights of Jura as you pedal.

On the other hand, that might be one challenge too many, so maybe just sit back, relax and open another book.

THE UPSIDE Small, friendly, midge-free beachside site miles from anywhere remotely touristy with decent facilities and a glorious ever-changing view out over the islands. Great for cyclists and canoeists.
THE DOWNSIDE Miles from anywhere remotely touristy, indeed miles from anywhere, and no mountains to climb.
THE DAMAGE Pitch from £8.50 per night; adults £1.75, children and dogs (must be on leads and no more than 2 at a time) £1.25; electric hook-ups £2.50.
THE FACILITIES Reasonable and well-maintained facilities that include toilets, showers, a laundry with coin-operated washing machines and tumble-dryers, as well as an iron and board.

There's also a small games room with pool and table-tennis tables.
NEAREST DECENT PUB The Argyll Hotel (01583 421212; www.argyllhotel.co.uk) at Bellochantuy, 5 miles south, is famous for being sprayed with machine-gun bullets by an aircraft just after the outbreak of the Second World War – it turned out to be an RAF plane testing its weaponry. It should be safe now, though, and has a good selection of food.
IF IT RAINS The ferries to Gigha, Islay, Colonsay, Arran (see www.calmac.co.uk for timetables and fares) and Jura (www.jurainfo.com) provide days out with a difference.
GETTING THERE Take the A82 from Glasgow, then the A83 through Inverary, Lochgilphead and

Tarbert. Muasdale is 25 miles south of Tarbert, alongside the A83. Alternatively, use the ferry from Gourock to Dunoon, then take the A815 north on to an unclassified road west to the A886, then the A8003 to Tighnabruaich and ferry from Portavadie to Tarbert, then the 25 miles south to Muasdale.
PUBLIC TRANSPORT A regular bus service from Glasgow passes the site, but it does take 4 hours! Traveline (08712 002233; www.travelinescotland.com) has details of times.
OPEN Easter–end Sept(ish).
IF IT'S FULL Nearest sites are Carradale Bay Caravan Park (01583 431665; www.carradalebay. com) or Machrihanish Caravan and Camping Park (01586 810366; www.campkintyre.com), but both have lots of statics and caravans.

Muasdale Holiday Park, Muasdale, Tarbert, Argyll PA29 6XD				
	t	01583 421207	w	www.muasdaleholidays.com	2	on the map

seal shore

Arran is geologically schizophrenic. It sits astride Scotland's Highland Boundary Fault, the geological feature that separates the rolling farmland of the Lowlands from the rugged peaks of the Highlands. So, when you disembark from the ferry at Brodick, which is appropriately in the middle of the island, you are faced with a choice.

Head north and you're off into the wilds of heather-clad mountains, roaming deer and deep-cut glens. Head south and you're into undulating countryside, standing stones and sea views. Luckily, Arran is not very big and is easily explored whichever way you choose. But if you have come to Arran more for heritage than for hiking, then south is the way to go.

Seal Shore, at Kildonan on the southern tip of Arran, has one of the island's very few sandy beaches. As the name suggests, it is best known for the abundance of sea life to be spotted bobbing among the waves and the birdlife gliding above them. The campsite is a neat and compact little place, run by a no-nonsense couple originally from Yorkshire. It slopes gently down to the beach, which has a handy finger of black rock, known as a dolerite dyke, protruding from the sands into the water. It's ideal for basking in the sun, as long as the seals (which may or may not be German) haven't already bagged the best spots.

The dolerite dyke is just one example of Arran's geological oddities. There are examples of rocks on Arran formed in virtually all the geological periods of the earth, from the Cambrian to the Triassic, making the isle a geologist's treasure trove.

Bounding forward a few million years in time, Arran still has plenty to offer those who haven't packed a rock hammer in their rucksack. Kildonan is the ideal base from which to explore the island's history, and its rich heritage is apparent in the very names of its attractions. Kildonan itself is named after St Donan, a 6th-century Irish monk who settled here. Out in the sound stands the lighthouse on Pladda, a Norse name meaning 'flat isle', while further in the distance is the gigantic hump of Ailsa Craig, whose name comes from the Gaelic for 'fairy rock'. Above the seashore stand the ruins of a 13th-century keep, first built by the MacDonald clan (or Lords of the Isles). More recently, Arran was known as Clydeside's playground because it attracted hordes of holidaying dockers on their annual holidays. Back then, sailing down the Clyde to Arran for the Trades' Fortnight was known as going 'doon the water'. Those days are long gone now, as are most of the shipyards on the Clyde, but that ages-old mix of Norse and Gaelic culture with Highland and Lowland Scottish history has left its mark here.

If you have the time then it's worth circumnavigating the island because the less-frequented western side has a number of attractions, not least the stone circle at Machrie and the faded grandeur of the Victorian Blackwaterfoot Lodge Hotel. And on the stretch of road from Lochranza in the north to Brodick you'll find one of Scotland's little slices of Cornwall: Corrie is a huddle of cottages along the road by a small harbour and is an ideal base for tackling Arran's most popular climb to the summit of Goat Fell. Its popularity lies not only in its relatively accessible summit, but also in its great vantage point to muse over the delights of this intriguing, schizophrenic little island.

THE UPSIDE Seabirds, seals and sandcastles.

THE DOWNSIDE The occasional howling souwesterly testing the resilience of your geodesic dome tent.

THE DAMAGE £6 per person, plus £1–4 (depending on size) for a camper van or tent. Tents larger than 6-person capacity aren't permitted due to the site's size. Children aged 5 and under are free and 6–15-year-olds are £3. Dogs are free.

THE FACILITIES Award-winning showers set in a neat and well-maintained whitewashed block (50p for the power showers, the older ones are free). Dishwashing area, laundry, baby-changing facilities and access to a fridge-freezer. There's also a new undercover (and windproof!) cooking area and campers' day room with freeview/sky. Chargers are available for mobile phones, cameras and the like.

NEAREST DECENT PUB The Kildonan Hotel (01770 820207; www.kildonanhotel.com) is right next door and serves excellent food in the restaurant (booking essential) and decent beer and bar fare. The view is great, too, looking out across the garden to the sea. Alternatively, there's the Pier Head Tavern (01770 600418) at Lamlash, dishing up fresh, home-cooked food in generous portions at bargain prices.

IF IT RAINS There is a small museum at Brodick and a range of craft shops in Lamlash. The Auchrannie Hotel Spa Resort (01770 302234) also has extensive leisure facilities including an impressive swimming pool (open to members of the public 11am–4:30pm and 7–9pm daily/ 8:30pm Sundays). For something different, try gorge-walking, wet and wild in its own right – involving climbing, scrambling, jumping and plunging and the odd bit of doggy-paddling up, down and around watery gorges – a bit of rain won't dampen the fun; 3-hour trips are operated by the Arran Adventure Company (01770 302244; www.arranadventure.com) for £40 a pop.

GETTING THERE From Brodick follow the B841 south for 12 miles. Turn left at the sign for Kildonan and follow the road down the hill towards the sea. The campsite is down a side road on the left, next door to the Kildonan Hotel.

PUBLIC TRANSPORT There is a bus service (no. 323) from Brodick Ferry that stops 45 metres from the site every few hours.

OPEN Mar–Oct.

IF IT'S FULL An extremely basic campsite with no hot water or showers lies at Glenrosa (01770 302380) just north of Brodick. There's no need to book, and it's £4 per person per night.

Seal Shore Camping & Touring Site, Kildonan, Isle of Arran KA27 8SE

| | t | 01770 820320 | w | www.campingarran.com | 3 | on the map |

marthrown of mabie

Huddled around a life-preserving fire that illuminated the gloom of their Iron-Age roundhouse, our ancestors eked out a living in places like Mabie Forest. Today you can follow in their footsteps in what has to be one of Europe's first reconstructed Iron-Age roundhouses that you can actually stay the night in. Get down and dirty and all elemental hunter-gatherer while cooking your own food over the fire, enjoying the pleasures of an al-fresco toilet and a dense and moody forest where little has changed over the last few millennia.

Marthrown is a special place in so many ways. The forest itself is awash with native Caledonian trees, with characterful old Scots pines each managing the wilful Scottish trick of being a different shape to the rest of their brood, as well as birch, rowan and juniper. Edging over the grassy mound that separates the heart of the 'multi-activity centre' from the roundhouse, you half expect to find a gaggle of Iron-Age hunters crowded around a clearing where Celtic songs and stories were once celebrated in wild ceilidhs.

Today, the roundhouse – an impressive construction that manages to stand up to the full might of the Atlantic weather systems sweeping in off the coast – is similarly full of life. Perfect for groups as it sleeps up to

16, it inevitably plays host to the occasional stag and hen party, and is also popular with groups of friends looking for something a bit different. And different it is: you camp around the central woodburner (in place of the old open fire, which ended up burning down the first reconstructed roundhouse, hence the safer alternative for roundhouse mark II), perfect for cooking up something tasty and keeping the place cosy. Just nearby is a canvas tipi and a Mongolian yurt, each of which have room enough to sleep four people, but the roundhouse is the real star. Tents are also welcome and it is possible to hire the whole site for exclusive use.

Rather than just sticking up the roundhouse and leaving it at that, the family team behind Marthrown has made an effort to recreate other earthy features, which fit neatly into today's vogue for all things clean and green. Rather than clog the local sewage system there is a simple but highly effective odour-free straw urinal as well as a compost toilet and an 'outdoor' shower. Luxurious extras include a sauna and hot pool that are free of charge for guests.

The surrounding forest, which is alive with red squirrels and woodpeckers, is one of the best locations in Scotland for mountain-biking. You can hire a bike from dedicated cycle centre 'the shed' (www.cycle-centre. com) just a mile away and explore the forest, which has been opened up as part of the excellent Seven Stanes programme (www.7stanes.gov.uk). All skill levels are catered for, with everything from easy and gently undulating forest trails that are perfect for beginners to some seriously testing 'black runs' that fling you and your wheels at high speed down through tough terrain with vaulting trees on either side.

At Marthrown itself there are two 12-metre climbing towers that offer low and high ropes, as well as the epic 'Leap of Faith', which has sorted the men from the boys on many a stag weekend (needs to be booked in advance). However you spend your day at Marthrown, the highlight is getting back around the stove. Whether you are in one big group or just sharing space with complete strangers there is a real sense of community and of getting back to basics. Taking a starlit stroll and then walking back to the welcoming and gently smoking arms of the simple dwelling is a strangely comforting experience that people have been enjoying for thousands of years.

THE UPSIDE Enjoy the simple life and cosy nights by the stove like your ancestors.

THE DOWNSIDE The extra £5 per night charge for campers to use the kitchen facilities.

THE DAMAGE £16 in low season to £19.50 in high per person in the roundhouse; 1–3-person tents £15; family tents £25. The Mongolian yurt costs £50 per weeknight and £110 per weekend night in low season and £60/£125 in high. Duvets, towels and sleeping bags are available. Furry canine friends are permitted.

THE FACILITIES Hot showers, a kitchen, sauna and hot pool. You can also get breakfast for £4.50 or a light brekkie for £3 and 3-course dinners for £11 (please book meals in advance). And for anyone who's about to tie the knot and wants a venue with a difference, then look no further than here, as Marthrown caters for weddings, too.

NEAREST DECENT PUB You will be spoilt for choice in Dumfries, 5 miles away. A couple of the best are the riverside Coach and Horses (01387 279754), which serves hearty pub grub, and the Hole in the Wall (01387 252770) – both serve lunch only, though, so if you're after a good evening meal head for the Linen Room (01387 255689; www.linenroom.com).

IF IT RAINS Stay in and stoke up the flames inside the wood-burner or visit the nearby town of Dumfries.

GETTING THERE Leave Dumfries on the A710 towards New Abbey. When you reach Islesteps look out for the right turn to Mabie Forest and Mabie House Hotel. When you come to the sign for Mabie House Hotel the road bears left and you will see signs for Marthrown of Mabie Education Centre. The site is a mile from here along a winding forest track.

PUBLIC TRANSPORT Bus no. 372 from Whitesands in Dumfries stops at the bottom of the road; from there it's a 1½-mile walk into the forest. If you have a heavy load, it's perhaps best to opt for a taxi from Dumfries.

OPEN All year.

IF IT'S FULL No roundhouse alternatives nearby; but Kirk Loch Caravan and Camping Site (07746 123783 – call between 5 and 6pm) occupies a great spot on the shores of Lochmaben, 12 miles away to the north-east.

Marthrown of Mabie, Mabie Forest, Dumfries DG2 8HB			
	t 01387 247900	w www.marthrown.com	4 on the map

blinkbonny wood

Everyone (apart from maybe Freddy Krueger and Goths) prefers sweet dreams to nightmares. For campers the dream is to arrive at a secluded wood, pitch up and have the place to yourself. Once the birds have gone to bed there's nothing but the rustle of the bracken and the odd falling pine cone to disturb your slumbers. And there's no worse camping nightmare than having the peaceful silence broken by a couple of backfiring vans arriving to disgorge a borstal-load of backpackers in the middle of the night.

Well, rest assured that won't happen at Blinkbonny Wood. This 100-acre woodland of mixed pine and broadleaf in East Lothian has only two small clearings in the bracken for a maximum of four tents at a time. And it's all so far from any road that you'd need a high-powered *Spooks*-style surveillance kit to detect any sound. You also have to leave your wheels at the gate and walk up the track for five minutes to find the site.

Each pitch has a stone fire pit and rough, wooden bench seats so you can cook and keep your bum dry at the same time. Just around the hill from the pitches sits a log cabin offering a snug vantage-point for spotting birdlife and deer. And if you look back towards Edinburgh, you can see the rump of Arthur's Seat rising into the sky.

The views from the pitches are none too shabby, either. They're a bit subtler, though, looking out over the soft farmland towards the sea, with the bird-splattered Bass Rock poking out of the water, and Traprain Law in the distance. The law is a large earthen mound, first used as a burial chamber in about 1500 BC and subsequently used as a fort before housing a Roman town. You can also see North Berwick Law, a 180-metre volcanic plug rather than an earthen mound, topped off by a replica pair of whales' jawbones (the real ones, which had been placed there in 1709, eventually rotted away and had to be replaced in 2005). Beyond all that is the sea, a bluey-grey sliver.

There are some great beaches on the East Lothian coast, from the massive dunes of Gullane to the gentler pleasures of Tyninghame, and some wonderful little villages like Athelstaneford, which sounds like something from the Domesday Book, and traditional towns like North Berwick and Dunbar, both solid and stoney and built to withstand the rigours of North-Sea winds. Further down the coast, out of sight, is another incongruously impressive site rising from the ground – the nuclear power station at Torness. Seen from the A1 across a yellow field, it looks rather pleasant and peaceful, its benign exterior hiding the fury that's going on in its core.

Luckily there's nothing quite so fierce or frantic going on at Blinkbonny Wood. The Wray family has owned the land since 2002, but they only began to take a few tents in 2007 and it remains something of a sideline. Steve Wray is a man of many parts. He grows his own lavender, which keeps the local bees

happy, and has a small workshop where he runs classes in such exotica as charcoal making and bird-box building. Around the back is the compost toilet and a marvellous vernacular greenhouse he built himself.

All of which leaves you in absolutely no doubt that this is a site for purists, a real back-to-nature adventure with limited home comforts. There's the compost toilet and that's about it: no showers, no running water and no electricity. Just you and the trees, the birds and the bees.

THE UPSIDE Quiet, secluded, virtually private camping in the rolling hills of East Lothian.
THE DOWNSIDE You need wellies as it can get a bit damp and muddy.
THE DAMAGE It's £5 per person per night (inclusive of firewood). Dogs are free but must be kept on a lead.
THE FACILITIES There's a compost toilet and each pitch comes with a gallon of fresh water (though not for drinking) and, as the old Hanna-Barbera cartoons used to say, 'That's all folks!'.
NEAREST DECENT PUB The weirdly named Goblin Ha' in Gifford (01620 810244) is a typical

small village pub with a handful of locals sneaking a pint in the middle of a weekday afternoon. Don't go for the bistro; head for the small cosy bar at the side of the hotel.
IF IT RAINS Visit the Pishwanton Wood Project (01620 810259; www.pishwanton.com), just up the road from the campsite. It's an environmental education centre, covering everything from bio-dynamics to herbal medicine.
GETTING THERE Come off the A1 at Haddington and follow the signs for Gifford. On entering the village turn right and drive through to a junction by the golf club. Turn left (for Long Yester). Follow

the road all the way until it seems to run out in a farmyard. There's a right turn up the hill but just past it, at the farm, is a hidden right turn. Take it and follow the road for half a mile or so and on the right is a clearing with a metal gate and a sign saying Blinkbonny Wood.
PUBLIC TRANSPORT The closest you can get by public transport is Gifford. There is a bus service to there but it's a 3½-mile walk to the site.
OPEN Apr–Oct.
IF IT'S FULL Not quite as woody, but in a lovely east-coast location is Lochhouses (p41).

Blinkbonny Wood, Long Yester, Nr Gifford, East Lothian EH41 4PL

| t | 01620 825034 | w | www.blinkbonnywood.com | 5 | on the map |

lochhouses

Lochhouses used to be the only Scottish outpost of the Featherdown Farms empire, the ubiquitous chain of sites for pampered campers who like their creature comforts, the chain about which everyone has an opinion. Like Marmite or Mandelson, you either love 'em or hate 'em, but there's no denying their success.

The Dale family who own the Lochhouses site took the decision to strike out on their own with a similar concept. You still get all the feathery and downy creature comforts you'd expect – fresh linen, clean towels, enough culinary gadgets to keep celebrity chefs amused for hours – but without all the complicated booking forms and extra charges for this, that and the next thing. And instead of the all-canvas tents of Featherdown, Lochhouses has similar-sized Estonian log cabins with canvas fronts. They're essentially the same thing, but the additional wooden infrastructure means that they can be kept warm enough to be occupied in the winter months.

The huge camping field at Lochhouses is a mile or so down a dirt track from the Dales' farmhouse, which is itself a good mile or so from a minor road, and it sits just beneath a sizeable dune that shields it from the sea winds. So, the only invading noises come from the whispering pine trees, the hens clucking about and the sound of ponies munching grass in the field next door.

The cabins are neatly placed around the periphery of the site, leaving plenty of privacy for campers and space in which to roam. By the entrance there's an old beached lobster-catcher boat that serves as a small tuckshop with basic provisions inside if you run short. After all, it's a long way back to civilisation from here.

Once you've settled in and fed the hens, go for a clamber up the dune to take in the views of the coast, from Bass Rock in the north down to the ruined castle of Dunbar on the promontory to the south. Dead ahead is an expanse of the North Sea with just the occasional passing cruise ship out on the horizon.

The south-east coast of Scotland must be the least visited part of a country that's always crawling with tourists. With the great aortic artery of the A1 slicing through the land perhaps it's no surprise that most folk coming from the south, from the Romans to the English armies, have made a beeline for Edinburgh without bothering to stop – unless, of course, there was a Scottish army standing in their way.

But there's a host of reasons to explore the stretch of coast from the border at Berwick, past St Abbs and Dunbar. There are cliffs, castles, sandy bays and battlefields and a Domesday directory of ancient villages.

And nowadays there's the John Muir Country Park to add to the list. Not as well known, even in Scotland, as he deserves to be – even though his books detailing his wilderness walks are still best-sellers – John Muir was a pioneer wilderness conservationist born in Dunbar in the 1830s. He emigrated to the United States and played a huge part in the establishment of national parks there, including the gem at Yosemite Valley. His memorial park in East Lothian is on a slightly smaller scale and doesn't have quite the same scenery but still stretches along several miles of the coast from the ruined castle at Dunbar, along Belhaven Bay (past the campsite) and on towards Bass Rock.

And it's all just a handy 45-minute drive from Edinburgh, which is probably where you were heading in the first place.

THE UPSIDE It's the same kind of Featherdown camping with all the creature comforts. Hurray! THE DOWNSIDE It's same kind of Featherdown camping with all the creature comforts. Boo! THE DAMAGE Prices are on a per cabin basis and range from £250 in low season to £350 in high for a long weekend and £350 in low season to £750 in high for a full week. There are no additional charges for linen or towels, which are included in the price. Dogs can accompany you free of charge. THE FACILITIES Ship-shape and Bristol fashion with 4 showers and WCs in a tidy block at the entrance to the field. There's also a beached lobster boat with a tuckshop inside for the basics.

NEAREST DECENT PUB There are 2 to choose from in East Linton. The typical red-brick Crown Hotel (01620 860335) has a good range of ales and whiskies and is a little 'Laura Ashley', while the Linton Hotel (01620 860202) is similarly smart. Both serve cracking meals. IF IT RAINS Take a trip to see Concorde at the National Museum of Flight (01312 474238; www.nms.ac.uk). GETTING THERE Come off the A1 by Haddington or Dunbar and take the A199 (it's the old A1 and runs parallel to the new road). Turn off on to the A198 at the signpost for Tyninghame and follow the straight road until you see the small sign for Lochhouses pointing up a track to the right (it's just before the road bends left). Follow the track all the way past some cottages and through the farmyard to the farmhouse. PUBLIC TRANSPORT There are regular trains on the main east-coast line stopping at Dunbar, from which there's a no. 120B bus service run by Eve Coaches (01368 865500) that passes by Tyninghame and Whitekirk, but it's a long walk from the road to the farm. OPEN All year. IF IT'S FULL Booking is essential. However, Blinkbonny Wood (p37) is a site on a 100-acre woodland south of Haddington, though it only has room for 4 pitches.

Lochhouses, Tyninghame, Nr Dunbar, East Lothian EH42 1XP

| t | 01620 870209 | 6 on the map |

gimme shelter

Take a couple of former hippies, a slice of fine Fife woodland and an old Rolling Stones number and what do you get? Probably all sorts of things, but Gimme Shelter is one of the less obvious outcomes to spring to mind.

Chris and Yvonne Barley have been here since the early seventies, having relocated from Yorkshire to this rustic bolthole near Dunfermline to start afresh. Over the years they've managed to extend the property to include a couple of cottages and, ultimately, the hilly woodland that forms the campsite. It's all surprisingly quiet and secluded given its position in prime commuting territory for Edinburgh. Admittedly you can just hear the M90 from some of the pitches, but elsewhere it's the Pinkerton Burn tumbling through the site that makes the most noise.

It hasn't always been this tranquil, though. This is the ancient Kingdom of Fife, dripping with history, much of it bloody. There was the Battle of Inverkeithing in 1651, one of the countless skirmishes after the English had invaded (again). It was Cromwell, this time, and he'd become pretty good by now so he and his New Model Army won at a canter.

There's an old story in these parts that, such was the slaughter, the Pinkerton Burn ran red for several days. Nice. But then, as aficionados of the Rolling Stones should know, 'Gimme Shelter' was a track on the album 'Let It Bleed'.

The only battle raging here now, though, is that old sixties chestnut: the Beatles versus the Stones. Take your pick, because the camping pitches dotted around the wood are all named after songs – 'Strawberry Fields', 'Rising Sun' and so on – so you'll have to come down on one side or the other.

In the site's upper pitches, out in the open and exposed to the blistering Fife sun, there's drinking water available in containers. Then in the lower pitches, which tend to be secluded arbours within the shade of all the trees, there's cold-running mains water.

Each of the pitches has its own wooden furniture (all hand-made by Chris) as well as a fire pit, the wherewithal for which is on sale at reception to get you going (kindling, paper, lighters and a bag of a logs), though you're free to add any burnable bits and bobs you can find lying around.

And it's such a mazy wood, with some of the pitches accessible only through narrow grassy strips fringed with encroaching woodland, that there's a real feeling of safety and seclusion, making it great for kids. Unless they're planning to machete their way through the woodland, the only way out is past their parents' tent.

When it's time to go exploring away from the site, Inverkeithing is less than a half-hour train ride from Edinburgh across the famous Forth Rail Bridge so taking the train is a hassle-free means of seeing Scotland's capital. Or if you fancy something a little less busy, take a trip up the Fife Coastal Road through a chain of fabulous old fishing villages such as Pittenweem, Elie and Crail all the way to St Andrews, the home of the Royal and Ancient Golf Club, founded in 1754. And if you want to go the whole hog, you can swing back through Dunfermline, another of Scotland's former capitals and proud birthplace of Andrew Carnegie, once the world's wealthiest man, and the more modest son of the manse, Gordon Brown.

Back at the Rolling Stones campsite, in exile from main street, you can shake your hips and tumble dice, shine a light and let it loose and you'll soon start to question whether you can't always get what you want.

THE UPSIDE Proper woodland camping with real wood fires.
THE DOWNSIDE Can get a bit messy after heavy rain and its minimal facilities make it more suitable for hard-core campers than newbies.
THE DAMAGE For the first night it's £6 per person (any age) plus £6 per car. From the second night onwards under-2s and cars are free.
THE FACILITIES There are various facilities areas around the site but they're pretty basic compost toilets with no showers. Drinking water is available, as is wood for fires. Down at the gallery there's a fridge-freezer and free wi-fi.
NEAREST DECENT PUB Go and sample the real ales at the Burgh Arms (01383 410384) on the High Street in Inverkeithing. It's traditional in the sense of having live music, a darts board and a pretty standard but keenly priced meal menu (lunches only).
IF IT RAINS Given that the site has no showers, take a trip to the Beacon Centre (01592 583383) swimming baths at Burntisland. It's a good opportunity to have a wash but there are flumes and a wave machine as well.
GETTING THERE Come off the M90 at Junction 1 (the first junction after the Forth Road Bridge if you're coming from Edinburgh). Following the signs for Inverkeithing on the A921 and go through the town. Just past the railway station turn left on to the B981 and follow the road for nearly a mile. The site entrance is signposted just before the road veers to the right.
PUBLIC TRANSPORT There are frequent trains to Inverkeithing from Edinburgh but it's a mile's walk to the site from the station.
OPEN All year.
IF IT'S FULL Fife's not really camping territory so always book with Gimme Shelter. In a jam, best to head north to either Comrie Croft (p63) or Ardgualich Farm (p73) – though they are both a bit of a distance away.

Woodland Camping Gimme Shelter, 2 Dales Farm Cottage, Duloch, Nr Dunfermline, Fife KY11 7HR

| t | 01383 417681 | w | www.woodlandcampinggimmeshelter.com | 7 | on the map |

easter drumquhassle farm

At a time when many farms are turning their backs on traditional farming in favour of more lucrative options like converting to farmstead housing or luxury flats, Easter Drumquhassle Farm makes a refreshing change. The animals around here are not just for show, with sheep being grazed as the main farming activity and horses also at livery at this 40-acre site. Making your way to the shower in the morning, you have as much chance of running into a waddling duck or clucking hen as you do a fellow camper.

As well as farming and camping, there's also a cosy B&B in one of the 19th-century farm buildings, a warm and welcome escape on a wet day. Most of the campers arriving here, however, are just happy to find anywhere to crash – Easter Drumquhassle Farm is a stopping point on the epic walk of the West Highland Way (see Walks and Wheel Trails feature, p88).

The West Highland Way, which runs past the campsite, is Scotland's most famous long-distance walk. Easter Drumquhassle Farm is a virtually obligatory stop for walkers, because, as a sign at the entrance so proudly points out, 'This is the only campsite in the Drymen area'. You can usually tell which way walkers have come, as those heading north from Glasgow will be nursing just a few first-day blisters and twinges, while those staggering in from the north will have a catalogue of aches and pains, and more than a few tall stories to tell after trekking all the way from Fort William.

The site is spread across a small grassy field, dotted with trees, which provide some shelter, but the ground can be quite hard in places, so bring a mallet and watch out for roots when pitching. The views are expansive, with rolling fields all around and the Kilpatrick Hills rising in the distance. The site itself offers a few creature comforts – the shower and toilet facilities are basic, but there is a rudimentary wet-weather shelter in an old barn and there are also two wigwams for those looking for a step up in luxury. The owners also offer the option of a cooked breakfast in the morning, a nourishing extra welcomed by many walkers.

Even for those not enthused by long walks, a quick stroll on the West Highland Way is practically compulsory at Drumquhassle. An easy option is to trek up the road a couple of miles north to the small town of Drymen, where a sprinkling of welcoming pubs brighten up the main square. The site owners offer lifts to and from the pub for the terminally lazy, though the walk is lovely on a balmy evening, slipping past fields with glimpses of Loch Lomond on one flank and the Campsie Fells on the other.

The name Drumquhassle comes from the Gaelic 'drum', meaning ridge, with the 'quhassle' referring to the Roman Fort on the hill near the campsite. The site has yet to be excavated, but you can troop up and take a look at the place where it stood marking the northern boundary of the Roman Empire.

Easter Drumquhassle will never win awards for its range of facilities, but if you're looking for an honest, relaxed site where you can kick back and watch the world go by, or launch yourself on to the West Highland Way, then it fits the bill.

You cannot fail to love a place where the only real downside is being woken up in the morning by an over-eager cockerel – and even that can be forgiven when you tuck into a hearty cooked breakfast, made with free-range eggs, in the old farmhouse.

THE UPSIDE Real farm feel and hearty cooked breakfasts that set you up for the day.
THE DOWNSIDE Facilities on the very basic side of adequate, but they are due to be upgraded (see below).
THE DAMAGE Tent £5 per night; wigwam £7 per night; whole wigwam £32. B&B £26 per person per night. Friends with wagging tails are also welcome, leads-on around the farm animals.
THE FACILITIES A wet-weather shelter with a small campers' kitchen area, toilets and hot shower. But permission has been granted and plans are underway to build a brand new toilet/shower block, as well as a small onsite shop and laundry (due to be finished at some point in October 2010).

NEAREST DECENT PUB The historic Clachan Inn (01360 660824) in Drymen, dating back to 1734, is just less than 2 miles away and serves up reliable pub grub and some excellent Scottish ales, including Belhaven Best.
IF IT RAINS The wet-weather shelter provides some respite, while the visitor centre complex with its shops, eateries and aquarium at Loch Lomond Shores (01389 751035; www.lochlomondshores.com) and the buzzing city of Glasgow are both an easy drive away.
GETTING THERE The campsite is a 30-minute drive from Stirling. Take the A811 west for 20 miles and then look out for a turning towards Gartness. The site is along the old Gartness Road and is signposted.

PUBLIC TRANSPORT There is no direct public transport to the site, though trains run from Glasgow Queen Street to Alexandria (www.nationalrail.co.uk), where you can connect with a local bus (no. 309) to Drymen run by McColl's Coaches (01389 754321).
OPEN All year.
IF IT'S FULL Another *Cool Camping* site, Beinglas Farm (p55), at the other end of Loch Lomond, isn't too far away. Alternatively, wild camp (see p160 for some handy wild camping dos and don'ts) by the shores of Loch Lomond in the marked site at the foot of the mountain at Rowardennan (no facilities).

Easter Drumquhassle Farm, Gartness Road, Drymen, By Loch Lomond, Stirlingshire G63 0DN

| | t | 01360 660597 | w | www.drymencamping.co.uk | 8 | on the map |

glendaruel

Glendaruel is a tree-huggers' paradise, and we were tempted to illustrate the point with a host of photos bursting with glamorous arboreal specimens in all sorts of alluring poses. You know the kind of thing – a curvy looking Ash blonde draped over the bonnet of a sports car; a scantily clad Swedish conifer surrounded by butch-looking broadleaf oaks; or a near-naked native standing aloof and apart. But it wouldn't really do the place justice, and there wasn't a sports car to be found anywhere anyway. Besides, it isn't all about the trees; just minutes after we arrived a young roe-deer appeared, followed by a black rabbit, brown rabbit and a red-haired rabbit. Bambi ran off at the sight of us, but all three Thumpers didn't seem at all bothered by humanity. Just as well that Elmer Fudd wasn't among us.

Glendaruel is a small (in terms of pitches, not acreage) park with a few statics hiding in the trees, room for a few campers and caravans and a large field for tents that rarely reaches full capacity. The whole site is contained within the grounds of a long-gone stately home, with a handsome collection of trees forming the attractive backdrop that brings us tree-huggers to a state of ecstasy.

The location, in the heart of the Cowal Peninsula, surrounded by big wooded hills, feels very remote, but access is easy via a short ferry crossing. It's an ideal site for young families, with facilities to make camping life very easy: a shop, games room, campers' kitchen-cum-dining-room and all that glorious forestry open for exploration, adventures and, of course, hugs.

THE UPSIDE The magnificent collection of mature trees and wildlife about the place, family-friendly facilities and glorious location.
THE DOWNSIDE The odd midge may make itself known, and rain can occasionally spoil play.
THE DAMAGE Tents/caravans/campers £10 per night; adults £3; children £1.50, under-3s free; backpacker with small tent £6. Dogs are free.
THE FACILITIES Decent facilities with toilets, showers, laundry, camper's kitchen and dining shelter, games room, shop and children's play area.
NEAREST DECENT PUB The Oystercatcher (01700 821229; www.theoystercatcher.co.uk) at

Otter Ferry, 7 miles away, is the nearest decent pub and restaurant, situated in a beautiful location. There are moorings, if you're of the boat set, and folk have even arrived here by seaplane. Slightly further away, but possibly quicker to reach, is the Colintraive Hotel (01700 841207; www.colintraivehotel.com) a traditional hunting-lodge hotel with public bar and restaurant.
IF IT RAINS Dunoon is 18 miles away and has a swimming pool, leisure centre, museum, golf course, cinema and tenpin bowling centre. A little nearer, and continuing the tree theme, the Benmore Botanic Garden (01369 706261; www.rbge.org.uk) claims to contain every tree

it is possible to grow in the mild climate of western Scotland, so is an essential place for tree-huggers. The nearby Isle of Bute has a host of civilised tourist attractions from the restored Victorian toilets, to the outrageous opulence of Mount Stuart (01700 503877; www.mountstuart. com),a Victorian gothic mansion.
GETTING THERE Ferries to Cowal (from Gourock to Dunoon) are frequent. Then follow the A815 north for 3 miles, the B926 west for 12 miles then the A886 north to the site.
OPEN Apr–end Oct.
IF IT'S FULL Nothing else around for miles, so best to book in advance.

Glendaruel Caravan and Camping Park, Glendaruel, Argyll PA22 3AB

| t | 01369 820267 | w | www.glendaruelcaravanpark.com | 9 | on the map |

beinglas farm

You don't *have* to don a pair of sturdy boots caked in mud and an impressive branded, hi-tech waterproof jacket, but they will certainly help you fit in at Beinglas. The site is located in ridiculously sublime scenery, just north of Britain's largest stretch of freshwater at Loch Lomond and is surrounded by brooding mountain peaks. It's pure walkers' heaven – but that doesn't mean there's no appeal for other visitors too.

The road access itself – a nerve-defying sharp right turn when heading north across the busy A82, and then over a bumpy bridge – is almost designed to put off non-walkers. A much better way to enter Beinglas is on the famous West Highland Way long-distance walk (see Walks and Wheel Trails, p88), with the campsite lying in Glenfalloch, 25 miles north of the southern start of the trail at Milngavie. Arrive early, whether you're walking or not, because although the large field that houses the site may hold up to 100 tents, it can fill up fast and the best spots go quickly in summer.

If taking on a stretch of the West Highland Way does not tempt you then there are numerous other hills and mountains nearby. The peak that gives the site its name, Ben Glas, is dramatic in its own right, and

rises just behind the site. The mountain that acts as a magnet for walkers from all over, though, is Ben Lomond. One of the Munro mountains, Ben Lomond makes an excellent starting climb (five to six hours up and down, with the 'tourist path' as easy as they come, though the usual mountain precautions apply). From the top of Ben Lomond you may well be bitten by the Munro-bagging bug (see Walks and Wheel Trails, p91) as you can see a fair few of them from there, though the thought that you still have another 282 of these mountains over 3000 feet to climb is quite a sobering one.

While the A82 is enough to put off even the most hardened of city cyclists, the countryside around Beinglas is perfect for touring by car. There are distilleries, visitor centres and what seems like yet another loch at every turn; Loch Lomond is just two miles south of the campsite. If you are into seafood, then the charms of the original Loch Fyne Seafood Restaurant (01499 600236; www.lochfyne.com) are less than an hour's drive away along the banks of the eponymous loch.

Back at the site, the social hub is the large amenity block that comes complete with a shop dishing out maps, first-aid kits and other walking paraphernalia, as well as an impressive wet-weather shelter that boasts a pool table, laundrette, pay phone, seating and cookers. There is also a bar, popular in the evenings with outdoor types recalling the day's adventures. Don't be surprised to see a live band stroll in for your entertainment if you're staying over a summer weekend. And when the sun deigns to come out and shine, the beer garden is just the place to sit and enjoy a pint before it sets behind the craggy peaks.

If the weather turns, there are four wigwams onsite, two large and two small, and B&B chalets tucked at the back of the campsite beneath the watchful eye of Ben Glas. These may provide the perfect sanctuary after a solid day's trekking in the hills, but if you want to fit in you might as well pitch in with the rest of the West Highland Way devotees and join in the fun down on the camping field, no matter how wild it gets. When you have walked so far to get here, you'll sleep well in any weather.

THE UPSIDE A paradise for walkers with the West Highland Way running right through the site and great scenery all around.

THE DOWNSIDE Truly treacherous turning for drivers heading north (see Getting There).

THE DAMAGE Camping costs £6 per person; wigwams £12 per person.

THE FACILITIES Hot showers, shop, bar serving food, and wet-weather shelter with cooking facilities and a pool table.

NEAREST DECENT PUB Stay onsite or head a little further afield to the famous Drovers Inn (01301 704234; www.thedroversinn.co.uk) in the same village of Inverarnan, where you'll find a surreal mix of tatty taxidermy, centuries-old interior design and kilt-sporting barmen. A lively atmosphere abounds, especially during the weekly live-music sessions, and the menu consists of standard pub fare such as burgers and scampi.

IF IT RAINS Make new friends and enjoy good food and Scottish ale in the onsite lounge bar and restaurant until the weather improves. Or unwind over a few rounds of pool in the camping shelter.

GETTING THERE Simply follow the A82 from Glasgow north towards Loch Lomond. The road cuts around the western flank; continue past the village of Luss and the campsite is signposted on the right with that horrible turning taking you across a small bridge into the site.

PUBLIC TRANSPORT Citylink (08705 505050) buses ply the A82 every day from Glasgow.

OPEN All year, except Christmas.

IF IT'S FULL Head over to the *Cool Camping* site at Easter Drumquhassle Farm (p49).

Beinglas Farm Campsite, Inverarnan, Loch Lomond, Dumbartonshire G83 7DX

| t | 01301 704281 | w | www.beinglascampsite.co.uk | 10 on the map |

loch tay highland lodges

There may be a trio of campsites dotted in quick succession along the western shores of Loch Tay, but only one of them has its own marina with the largest teaching fleet of open-keel sailing dinghies in Scotland, a flotilla of Canadian canoes and plenty of other water sports opportunities including RIB (rigid inflatable boat) trips and fishing-boat hire. And there's a putting green, plus a bar and restaurant with waterfront terrace. You certainly won't be short of things to do at Loch Tay.

The site of Loch Tay Highland Lodges sits right on the loch and spreads across a 140-acre estate, most of which is occupied by holiday-park-style wooden lodges, but there's also a small campsite – tucked away, back up the hill overlooking the loch, a safe distance from the wooden lodges. As well as half-a-dozen tent pitches there are also wigwams and even heated wooden tipis on the campsite: green-painted pyramids that look quite organic and low-impact from the outside, but with interiors styled on a cheap B&B. They come as either 'standard' with TVs and fridges, or 'standard plus' with their very own kitchenettes and showers.

Whether you stay in a tent or attempt to seek refuge from the midges in a wigwam or tipi, you'll probably spend most of your time outdoors anyway, with all that's on offer. Water-based options include learning to sail on the loch, hiring a sailing dinghy or joining an organised kayak trip to the village of Killin, where a minibus will pick you up to save you the effort of paddling back against the wind. You can also rent a boat and buy a fishing permit in order to bring back some nice, juicy salmon or trout for dinner.

On land, a fleet of mountain and hybrid bikes awaits, with organised trips around the surrounding countryside. Adrenaline junkies will jump at the chance to be dropped off in the hills to return via speedy downhills on a 20-mile thrill ride. For those seeking a slower pace, you can also hire tandem hybrid bikes and children's bicycles. Then there's the 18-hole putting green, an archery range and clay-pigeon shooting, allowing you to savour the experience of blowing up clays over the silvery waters of Loch Tay.

One of the main attractions of this region, though, doesn't cost a penny and is what lures most people here – the panorama of rugged mountains and shimmering lochs that vault all around. Climbers and walkers will want to head up the slopes of Ben Lawers, a monster of a mountain at about 1350 metres, whose summit affords stunning views of numerous other Scottish peaks.

If all these action-packed activities leave you in need of something a touch more pedestrian, then a visit to the village of Fortingall will reveal the oldest yew tree in Europe, believed to be between 3,000 and 5,000 years old. Although the tree predates the adjacent church by millennia, it is fitting that a house of prayer should have been erected there, as yew trees are traditionally associated with religious worship. Sadly, the authorities were forced to construct a protective wall around the elderly yew to prevent tourists from snipping off twigs and branches.

Whether it's marvelling at ancient trees, crashing downhill on a mountain bike, having your first go at sailing or trying your hand at putting as well as Tiger, Loch Tay has it all. But none of these activities would be here if the loch wasn't a gloriously beautiful place to visit in its own right. And that can be appreciated with the minimum of effort – just a few steps from your tent.

THE UPSIDE There is enough here to keep you occupied for a week, both in the water and out.
THE DOWNSIDE A few too many lodges dotted around the hillside, and (if they haven't built the new block before you read this) the facilities aren't the best.
THE DAMAGE They have room for up to 15 tents. £15 per night for a small tent (up to 4-man size), larger tents are £18 per night. The unserviced wooden tipis cost £28 per night for 2, serviced ones £40. Wigwams are £32 per night for 2 (they are unserviced but have a fridge, kettle and microwave). Each tipi also has a meter for electricity. Four-legged companions free.
THE FACILITIES There's a toilet and shower block nearby and you can use the facilities at the marina without charge. Plans are underway for the building of a brand new state-of-the-art facilities block at some point in 2010, along with plans for 8 new octagonal woodland cabins complete with wood-burners, kitchens, shower rooms and views of Ben Lawers; as well as another 12 wigwams situated in a woodland copse.
NEAREST DECENT PUB The onsite Boat House (01567 820853) was purpose built to take advantage of the loch views with a wooden deck overlooking the marina. It serves bar meals, pizza and pre-ordered packed lunches.
IF IT RAINS Make the journey to the other side of the loch to the Ardeonaig Hotel & Restaurant (01567 820400), to enjoy the finest burgers in this part of Scotland as well as the huge steaks on the bistro menu. Unfortunately the bistro finishes serving food at 3pm. The restaurant is a more 'fine dining' experience and booking is advisable because it fills up fast.
GETTING THERE From the M9 take the A84 to Callander. Continue north from Lochearnhead on the A85 before turning right on the A827 to Killin. Continue through the village and the campsite is signposted to the right after a couple of miles.
PUBLIC TRANSPORT Caber Coaches (01887 820090) operate a bus service (no. 893) from Aberfeldy to Morenish. The campsite is 10 minutes' walk from the Morenish bus stop.
OPEN All year.
IF IT'S FULL The onsite lodges can be booked (for a minimum of 3 nights) and the tipis and wigwams are also on hand. Alternatively, Cruachan Farm (01567 820302) is just a stone's throw west on the road back to Killin.

Loch Tay Highland Lodges, Milton Morenish Estate, By Killin, Perthshire FK21 8TY

| t | 01567 820323 | w | www.lochtay-vacations.co.uk | 11 | on the map |

comrie croft

Comrie Croft is the very model of a modish modern campsite – it's new and environmentally friendly, it combines secluded woodland pitches with a camping field for families, it allows campfires and has a communal fire pit sheltered from the elements by a massive military cargo-chute where you can all sit around and get to know your neighbours.

The family camping field is limited to 12 tents at a time, so you're never crossing guy ropes with the campers next door, and there are a further 13 pitches dotted up in the woodland, along with three kåtas. These Swedish tipi-style tents are set on wooden decking and are large enough to house a family of six. They come equipped with sheepskin rugs, hand-crafted furniture and a bunch of logs for the wood-burning stove. Most of the pitches up on the hill are hidden from the others by trees and bracken, so you can feel like you have the place to yourself, but the price of all that woodland tranquillity is that vehicles have to be left at reception. Best, then, to come for a week to make it worthwhile humping all your gear through the forest.

Mind you, it's a small price to pay to camp in such glorious surroundings. A little pond above the wood is fed by a stream at one end, which spills out from the other side of the pond and burbles down through the wood. In the evening the sound of the water vies with the crackle of campfires and roasting sausages, while the rising smoke helps keep any winged monsters at bay.

The nearby town of Crieff is something of a one-street tourist affair and if you fancy reacquainting yourself with town living you're better off going the extra mile to Perth, a delightful product of the Georgian enthusiasm for the neo-classical. It's all far grander than a wee town on the banks of the Tay deserves, but then that's its unique appeal. It also has quite some history behind it, being a former capital of Scotland and close to Scone Palace, the coronation site of ancient Scottish kings. There's a replica here of the Stone of Destiny, the coronation stone on which new monarchs would sit to be crowned. The original was 'borrowed' by Edward I and taken to Westminster and has been used to crown English and British kings ever since. It was stolen in the 1950s by some enterprising Scottish students and, although it was recovered and returned to Westminster, rumours have always persisted that the stone they handed back was a replica they'd made and that the real one is still secreted away somewhere in Scotland for safe keeping. So when, after Scottish

Devolution, the Westminster Stone of Destiny was returned to Scotland permanently, no one knew if it was the real deal or not.

There's no doubting the authenticity of Comrie Croft, though. This is pretty much how modern camping should be and makes an ideal introduction if you're just setting out on a canvas adventure. It's also a painless way of easing yourself into Scotland. This part of Perthshire's pretty well-heeled, a land of gentleman farmers and classy spas and a far cry from the more rugged landscapes as you head north up the A9 past Pitlochry. But then not everyone wants the full-on lochs and heather experience. At least not at first. Cut your teeth on the sloping fields and woods of central Perthshire and you'll soon be raring to branch out into the wilder stuff. Or perhaps you'll find that Comrie Croft's just the kind of thing you've been looking for all these years and decide you don't need to take another step. And who can blame you?

THE UPSIDE Modish modern camping in a peaceful woodland setting.

THE DOWNSIDE Its location is betwixt and between – east of the Trossachs National Park, south of the Grampians and west of Perth.

THE DAMAGE It's £7 per adult/£3.50 per child under 16 on a weeknight and £9/£4.50 on Friday and Saturday nights (these prices apply on weeknights in Jul and Aug too). Under-5s are free. The kåtas start at £45 for a single weeknight up to £299 for a week's stay in high season. Well-behaved dogs are welcome and cost nothing.

THE FACILITIES Spotlessly fresh. A block with 3 powerful showers and 2 WCs, and outside are dishwashing and recycling facilities. There's a shop at reception (with another couple of WCs) where you can buy firewood at £5 per large bag and basics like milk. There's also a fresh drinking-water tap and 24-hour tea and coffee machine. Mountain bikes are available to hire as well.

NEAREST DECENT PUB The Royal (01764 679200) in Comrie. Part of the Royal Hotel, it's towards the end of the main street in a little square on the right. Choose between the hotel's posh bar or the more pubby affair at the side.

IF IT RAINS Although it's a bit of a drive, visit Scone Palace (01738 552300; www.scone-palace. net), just north of Perth. It's where Scotland's ancient kings were crowned and is the original home of the contentious Stone of Destiny. There's a replica here now, the real one being in Edinburgh. Or so they'd have you believe.

GETTING THERE Simple. It's directly off the A85 between Crieff and Comrie. There's a signpost for the track up the hill.

PUBLIC TRANSPORT Bus nos. 15 and 15A come from Perth and stop right opposite the site entrance. Coming the other way there are cross-country coaches from Oban via Crianlarich that run from May–Oct.

OPEN All year.

IF IT'S FULL There is a bunkhouse at Comrie Croft but for another campsite it's best to head to Ardgualich Farm (p73).

Comrie Croft, Braincroft, Crieff, Perthshire PH7 4JZ

| | t | 01764 670140 | w | www.comriecroft.com | 12 on the map |

glengoulandie

On arrival at Glengoulandie Campsite, you can expect the sort of welcome you only get at a small, family-owned site. This warmest of welcomes may have something to do with the fact that there are more deer in this part of the world than people. But, set amid the rolling hills and cobalt blue lochs of Perthshire and in the shadow of one of Scotland's most striking mountains – the legendary Schiehallion – this semi-solitary location has an obvious, scenic advantage.

The site at Glengoulandie nestles at the foot of another hill – Dùn Coillich – and is fringed by a trickling burn and a deer farm. If you're camping you can easily turn your back on the static caravans at the rear of the site, and when the campsite is busy the staff are sensitive enough to try to pitch families and non-families separately. This hands-on approach reflects the pride that's taken in the campsite; a pride that has fuelled Glengoulandie's environmentally minded ethos. Only eco-friendly products are used here, and they also operate a bio-sewage system and recycle as much waste as is humanly possible.

Within the campsite there is plenty to keep you occupied, with an onsite shop and café and a deer farm (campers can walk around here free of charge, but a more fun alternative is to hire the park's 4x4 and go for a spin). There's also a modest-sized fly-fishing lochan (small lake) brimming with rainbow and brown trout. The Land Registry asked the Glengoulandie folk what they wanted to call their lake, so they are hoping that Loch Coillich will soon appear on official maps. In the shop you can also buy postcards reproduced from photographs (taken by one of the site's staff members) of the park's Highland cattle – those cute furry ones – deer, ducks, peacocks and chickens.

Walkers are lured to the campsite by Schiehallion, the 'Fairy Hill of the Caledonians', a hulking and threatening-looking conical mountain that towers to over 1000 metres. Despite an ascent that is both steep and tiring, this is one of the easiest and most rewarding Munro ascents for those properly equipped. Schiehallion's location also cuts down on the travelling time for 'Munro baggers' (see Walks and Wheel Trails, p91), the mad souls determined to summit all of Scotland's 283 peaks over 3000 feet high before they die. The main path starts at the Braes of Foss car park, but the more adventurous walker can try to summit from the campsite – just be warned that the route is rather overgrown.

On a clear day atop Schiehallion, all the 'it feels like you are on top of the world' clichés ring true. You can see Loch Rannoch, Rannoch Moor, Loch Tummel and the lower hills of the Central Highlands. If you have no interest in tackling Schiehallion, though, it is notable for another reason. In the 18th century, the Astronomer-Royal hiked up the mountain in a bid to learn about the earth's mass; an expedition that was central to the development of map contours. So in some respects, the maps we all use today owe a great debt to Schiehallion.

Dùn Coillich itself is also unique. The 1,100-acre hill has been owned by the Highland Perthshire Communities Land Trust since January 2002, as a result of the first successful community land buy-out in the region. You can ramble around the hill, looking out for the 70 bird species, including golden eagles, and see the fledgling restoration of the rowan, birch and willow forest, with the first of 30,000 saplings planted at the end of 2005. This is exactly the sort of sustainable approach approved of by most visitors to Glengoulandie.

THE UPSIDE Camp among the hills and mountains of Perthshire and share a site with deer.
THE DOWNSIDE Home to around two-dozen static caravans.
THE DAMAGE Fees depend on the size of your tent and range from £10 for a 1–2-person tent to £16 for an 8–10-person tent. Dogs are welcome but must be kept on leads at all times and aren't permitted into the deer park.
THE FACILITIES Laundry, café, shop selling basic necessities (you can order basics such as newspapers, milk and rolls the night before and they'll be fetched from town the next day), hot showers and toilets.

NEAREST DECENT PUB It's a long walk (7 miles) to the nearest decent pub, the Ailean Chraggan (01887 820346), which is located on the road towards Aberfeldy in Weem. You'll be rewarded with innovative fish and game dishes, as well as views over Loch Tay.
IF IT RAINS Head for Dewar's World of Whisky (01887 822010) in Aberfeldy and learn all about how whisky is made on the distillery tour, or hit their bottle shop to invest in a 12-year-old Aberfeldy single malt.
GETTING THERE Heading north from Edinburgh on the M90/A9 towards Inverness, take the A827 towards Aberfeldy and then the B846 towards

Kinloch Rannoch; the campsite is located 9 miles along this road.
PUBLIC TRANSPORT Stagecoach Perth (01738 629339) runs buses from Perth to Aberfeldy every hour and a quarter. From Aberfeldy, the Broons Buses and Taxis' (01882 632331) service to Kinloch Rannoch goes past the campsite, but only during school terms.
OPEN Easter–mid Oct.
IF IT'S FULL Other good campsites in the region include Ardgualich Farm (p73) or the Scottish Canoe Association campsite at Grandtully (www.canoescotland.com).

Glengoulandie Campsite, Glengoulandie Country Park, By Pitlochry, Perthshire PH16 5NL

| t | 01887 830495 | w | www.glengoulandie.co.uk | 13 | on the map |

ardgualich farm

Ardgualich Farm is one of those rough-around-the-edges anachronisms you cannot help but like. The simple site has been run by the same family since the Second World War came to a close in 1945 and has somehow managed to rumble on into the 21st century still enjoying the epic scenery that first lured Queen Victoria to Loch Tummel back in the 19th century.

Queen Victoria fell in love with Loch Tummel to such an extent that she would scarcely let a trip to her beloved Scotland pass by without visiting at least once. Today, the spot where she used to regally perch and survey the silvery shadow of the loch as it drifted off from Perthshire towards the Highland peaks in the north-west is fittingly dubbed the 'Queen's View' (though not, as you may think, for Victoria, but probably for Robert the Bruce's wife, Queen Isabella, who used to rest in nearby woods when she was out and about doing royal things in the 14th century) and comes complete with a swish visitor centre.

With numerous whisky distilleries nearby, world-class salmon and succulent local beef all wrapped around heather-clad hills and mountains, it is easy to see why any queen in any century with a penchant for living the good life was drawn here.

Tales of world-famous monarchs seem a long way away at Ardgualich Farm, just down the road from the viewpoint. To say the site has no pretensions is as obvious as saying that Holland is a bit short on ski slopes. The old farm has been joined on its rumble down the grassy hillside towards the loch by a collage of caravans and some static homes, but there is still plenty of room for campers, who enjoy some of the best views from their grassy pitches. There is a family-orientated field near the reception, but head right down the hill for the best spots. You can pitch your tent in the soft verges that fringe Loch Tummel, with only the sinewy sandy beaches and the lapping waves for company.

While sitting by the water's edge is enough for some, others choose to get in – and not just those brave enough to risk a swim in the bracing loch. Campers are encouraged to bring their own small boats or canoes, though jet skis are mercifully banned. There is no launch charge at Ardgualich, leaving you free to explore the nooks and crannies of Loch Tummel at your own pace. Campers can also enjoy a free fishing permit. After a day spent reeling them in, you can explore your primitive hunter-gatherer instincts and feast on freshly caught barbecued fish, with the world of mobile phones and tortuous commutes feeling far away indeed.

Some of Loch Tummel's most famous inhabitants can be found above it rather than in it. Ospreys are now thriving around the shores of the loch after years of decline, when the very survival of these impressive birds of prey in Scotland was in doubt. Other flourishing residents you are likely to encounter are roe deer, who have been known to slip into the site and startle campers who wake to discover them nosing around in their breakfast supplies.

Today Ardgualich Farm may not exactly have the facilities and luxuries fit for a queen. But what it does offer is a stripped-down camping experience with regal loch views, where you can get back to basics and barbecue your own fish as you idle your time away admiring the scenery and the wildlife right by the edge of the loch. Queen Victoria's ghost, as it wistfully haunts the hills above, will no doubt be ever-so-slightly jealous.

THE UPSIDE A queen's view for much less than a king's ransom.

THE DOWNSIDE Caravans and statics dot the site but aren't too intrusive and are kept away from the lochside.

THE DAMAGE £12 for a 2-person tent and £15 for a large family tent plus 50p for each extra person. Dogs are fine as long as they're on a lead.

THE FACILITIES There is a new toilet block with hot showers. It's a bit 'Portakabin', but is perfectly fine.

NEAREST DECENT PUB The Loch Tummel Inn (01882 634272) is an old-fashioned pub with a beer garden that overlooks the loch. Choose from the informal bar or loch-view restaurant. The home-made beef burgers and seared Shetland salmon are both highly recommended. It also serves a range of good ales and whiskies.

IF IT RAINS Pop into the Queen's View Visitor Centre to watch the short film about the area and then enjoy a pot of tea and a chinwag.

GETTING THERE Heading north on the A9 from Perth towards Inverness take the B8019 exit towards Killiecrankie. Turn left for Tummel Bridge (you're still on the B8019) and follow the road for 6 miles. The entrance to the campsite is on the left.

PUBLIC TRANSPORT The Pitlochry to Kinloch Rannoch bus (no. 82) operated by Broons Buses and Taxis (01882 632331) goes past the campsite 3 times a day (4 times on a Saturday).

OPEN Mar–Oct.

IF IT'S FULL Other Cool Camping sites are located at Glengoulandie (p69) and Loch Tay (p59).

Ardgualich Farm & Loch Tummel Caravan Park, Ardgualich, Pitlochry, Perthshire PH16 5NS

t | 01796 47282 | 14 on the map

caolasnacon

When the weather is perfect and you're pitched on the lochside edge of this campsite, sitting next to a campfire, looking across the rippling waters and out over the magnificent Mamore Mountains, it's hard to imagine camping life getting much better than this.

The site is situated at the shores of Loch Leven, where this long seawater inlet narrows, halfway between the more open waters of Loch Linnhe and the spot where the mountains bar the tides any further progress at the village of Kinlochleven. From the small promontory on which the lower half (and main camping area) of Caolasnacon lies, the view is made up entirely of a heady mix of mountains, trees, water and a bit of sky. The usual West Highland midge warning applies here, but the exposed lochside pitches don't suffer as badly as those even a few metres inland.

A glorious scene, then, and one would assume life really couldn't get any better – but it can, and has. During one of our *Cool Camping* stays here – at that gloriously still point in the evening when the fire had died and shadows began lengthening as the sun slipped away – a family of otters emerged from the seaweed and undergrowth on the margins of the loch. We had to rub the disbelief from our eyes before watching them play happily in the shallows for more than an hour, barely 10 metres from us. Whether it was familiarity with campers, our instinctive stillness or just good luck, we know not, but at one stage, those three otters got within a few steps of where we sat gazing at them.

These squeak-emitting little web-toed critters aren't the only wildlife to be spotted around this scenic idyll, though. Come morning and the sky is alive with buzzards soaring across the loch, while resident golden eagles patrol the mountain slopes behind the site. The usual signs of human activity feel a safe distance away – no traffic within view or earshot and no people around, except for fellow campers who feel similarly privileged to be taking up part of this untouched landscape – giving off a real sense of isolation in the wilderness.

With all this surrounding natural beauty, you could be forgiven for thinking that Caolasnacon is buried away hundreds of miles from anywhere else and therefore near-impossible to reach, but it isn't; the main road from Glasgow to Fort William is handily just three miles away, at Glencoe.

Besides wildlife-watching, this site offers a chance to completely immerse yourself in one of the most beautiful places in Europe, and an opportunity to traverse some of Britain's most exciting mountains. The Mamores, directly across Loch Leven from the campsite, are a wonderful walking place, while directly behind the site are the fearful rock walls of Glen Coe, where a steady head and two sure feet are a necessity. Canoeing in Loch Leven provides a different view of this scenic overload, and bikers will go pedal-mad for the route around the loch.

Within striking distance by car, on surprisingly good roads, are tourist centres such as Fort William and Oban, where distractions by boat (from Oban) and train (from Fort William) offer alternative or wet-weather entertainment. The Scottish Sealife Sanctuary also provides an insight into what goes on deep in the loch that washes those beautiful shores just metres from your tent.

Caolasnacon provides a unique opportunity to get away from it all, among some of the most appealing and least spoilt scenery in the land but, amazingly, remains within easy reach of all those modern conveniences that make camping life enjoyable, whatever the weather has in store.

THE UPSIDE Lovely lochside location in classic Highland scenery, and convenient for the main road south.

THE DOWNSIDE None, besides the usual midge warning.

THE DAMAGE From £10 for a 2-person tent and occupants, to £15 for a family.

THE FACILITIES Not the most modern, but decent enough, with free showers, toilets, washbasins, washing-up sinks, laundry and electric hook-ups. Gas can be obtained at the farm. Undercover chemical disposal point.

NEAREST DECENT PUB There is a good choice in Kinlochleven (3 miles) depending on what you're looking for: Bothan Bar (01855 831100) open from 4pm, in the Ice Factor, is quite trendy, with appropriate food; MacDonald's (01855 831539), not to be confused with the fast-food joint, offers traditional hotel fare as well as packed lunches for walks; the Tail Race Inn (01855 831772) is a simple pub doing simple food. Lochleven Seafood Café (01855 821048), on the other side of the loch, offers an excellent selection of fresh and fulsome fish.

IF IT RAINS The Ice Factor in nearby Kinlochleven has climbing walls, and the Scottish Sealife Sanctuary (01631 720386; www.sealsanctuary.co.uk) near Loch Creran to the south is superb. Fort William is a 30-minute drive.

GETTING THERE From the A82 (Glasgow–Fort William road), take the B863 (right) in Glencoe, signposted to Kinlochleven. The site is 3 miles further on the left.

PUBLIC TRANSPORT Highland Country's (01463 222244) no. 44 bus runs between Fort William and Kinlochleven.

OPEN Easter–Oct.

IF IT'S FULL Good options nearby include Blackwater Hostel and Campsite (01855 831253; www.blackwaterhostel.co.uk) in Kinlochleven, and the Red Squirrel Campsite (p83) in Glencoe.

Caolasnacon Caravan & Camping Park, Kinlochleven, Argyll PH50 4RJ

| t | 01855 831279 | w | www.kinlochlevencaravans.com | 15 | on the map |

red squirrel

Some people come to Scotland to delve deep into the country's rich and brutal history; others to traverse and climb its spectacular mountains – many of which are some of Europe's finest – while still more come just to enjoy a wee dram in the place where whisky began. If you fall into any of these categories, or ideally all three, the Red Squirrel campsite is the place for you. It's a cosy place, dwarfed by a phalanx of towering highland peaks in a glen draped in bloody history and home to one of Scotland's most famous pubs, where whisky-drinking is practically obligatory.

The Red Squirrel lies in Glencoe, many Scots' favourite glen, which is praise indeed in a country that overflows with epic scenery. From the moment you begin the descent from the barren wastelands of Rannoch Moor, it's clear you're approaching somewhere special, as the road dips to acknowledge huge glacial massifs on either flank. If you're not an experienced walker, then this is foreboding stuff, as your eyes are drawn skywards, up scree-shattered slopes that appear infinite as they disappear into the high clouds. The visitor centre in the glen organises walks for those not keen on heading out on their own; but if you have the right gear, knowledge and experience,

check the weather forecast and you can just set off on one of the myriad hikes and climbs that break off in every direction.

The campsite is also perfect for those who enjoy mountains from a purely sedentary position. On a sunny day you can just laze around this grassy site, which spreads across 20 acres of meadow and woodland with a couple of burns snaking through it. The Red Squirrel describes itself as a 'casual farm site' and casual it is indeed, with no official pitches. Push through to the end of the camp and follow the overgrown trail (you'll think you have gone the wrong way) and you can pitch on an isolated island with great views. Elsewhere, a freshwater pool sits invitingly, awaiting any camper brave enough to take the plunge and enjoy an envigorating swim. Another plus is that in specific spots the Red Squirrel allows open fires, though not after 11pm, when a silence rule descends on the camp.

The scene in Glencoe may be idyllic today, but, in the hazy morning mist of February 13, 1692, it was smeared with blood and terror. Talk to any member of the MacDonald clan and it may as well have been yesterday, for the pain they feel still simmers just below the surface. The government in

London had long wanted to 'deal' with the troublesome MacDonalds and saw their chance when the clan did not sign a compulsory oath of allegiance to the king in time. They employed the Campbells of Glen Lyon, who arrived to seek shelter and enjoy the hospitality of the MacDonalds (in time-honoured Celtic tradition). On the fateful morning, they carried out their orders and massacred as many MacDonald men, women and children as they could lay their swords and daggers on; any bedraggled survivors were left to wander off into the mountains through a descending blizzard.

After a hard day walking in the hills, or a sombre one visiting the massacre memorial and the visitor centre that illuminates the glen's history, most campers seek refuge in the welcoming arms of the legendary Clachaig Inn. A sign at the door bans 'Hawkers and Campbells' and this is deadly serious – history in this part of the world is strictly of the living variety. All other visitors, though, are welcomed through the door and into the bar like long-lost cousins and are soon enveloped in a world of tall stories, live music and more than one or two wee drams.

THE UPSIDE Epic mountain scenery laced with human drama.

THE DOWNSIDE The toilets are not the best, especially during the busy summer season.

THE DAMAGE £7.50 per person and children under 12 cost 50p.

THE FACILITIES Simple toilet block with hot showers (50p meter showers and hairdryers), water taps dotted around the site and a small information booth. Further toilets are scattered around the site, but you need to ask for them to be opened. There's a designated family area so kid campers can get to know one another and head off for adventures among the trees.

NEAREST DECENT PUB The legendary Clachaig Inn (01855 811252) is staggering distance up the road back towards Glencoe. The Boots Bar is the place to be if you've just come off the hills covered head to foot in mud. The main lounge bar is a more comfortable spot with views out of the large windows; both serve hearty walker-friendly food like wild boar burgers, with regular music on Friday and Saturday nights throughout the summer.

IF IT RAINS Learn about the nature and history of one of the most spectacular glens in Scotland at the Glencoe Visitor Centre (08444 932222). The home-baked cakes on sale in the coffee shop are divine.

GETTING THERE Head north on the A82 from Stirling towards Fort William. About three-quarters of the way down Glencoe a right turn is signposted 'Clachaig Inn'. Follow this single track down past the inn to the campsite.

PUBLIC TRANSPORT Scottish Citylink (08705 505050) services (either bus no. 914 or 915, depending on when you're travelling) from Glasgow stop at the Glencoe Visitor Centre.

OPEN All year.

IF IT'S FULL Unfortunately, the youth hostel down the road has closed its small camping site, so it's just the bunkhouse available now. Invercoe Highland Holidays (01855 811210), a few miles away, is a far more landscaped/corporate site, but has gorgeous loch views.

Red Squirrel Campsite, Glencoe, Argyll PH49 4HX

| t | 01855 811256 | w | www.redsquirrelcampsite.com | 16 | on the map |

Walks and Wheel Trails

Don a mac and a sturdy pair of brogues and head for the open road to experience the best of outdoor Scotland.

There's nothing you can say in mitigation of the midge and, sure it can rain like a leaky pipe here, but there's nowhere quite like Scotland when it's time to come out to play. Whether you want to walk, run, cycle or (whisper it) drive, there's somewhere beckoning you on in this scenery-laden country.

With mountains and lochs in plentiful supply and some of the most sparsely populated countryside in Europe to be found in the extreme north, this heather-strewn land is just the place to release your inner nomad on a long-distance path, tackle a famous Munro mountain or take a more cultured approach and follow a whisky trail.

Whatever your tipple, though, a word of warning: weather conditions can change in a flash, so always be prepared. In Scottish terms, that means take a can of Irn-Bru.

West Highland Way

This 95-mile schlep is the most famous walk in Scotland. Combining old drove roads, used to transport cattle, General Wade's 18th-century military roads and railway branch lines axed by Doctor Beeching in the sixties, it starts in Milngavie (don't ask why but it's pronounced 'mull-guy'), a northern suburb of Glasgow. It takes you through a tick list of Scottishness as you walk the length of Loch Lomond, cross the mighty Rannoch Moor, peer into dark Glencoe and end up passing Ben Nevis before collapsing in a heap on reaching Fort William. Open since 1980, it's the feather in the cap of any serious Scottish walker.

www.west-highland-way.co.uk

Durness to Kinlochbervie via Cape Wrath

If the West Highland Way's the M1 of Scottish walks, this is the B999. Take the ferry across the Kyle of Durness and the minibus to Cape Wrath, the north-west point of the mainland. Then walk down the cliffy coast of the Parph, miles and miles from anywhere, until you reach the breathtaking Sandwood Bay, surely the most remote beach in Britain, before carrying on over the moorland to finish at Kinlochbervie. This walk is seriously remote, so don't leave home without proper kit and the Ordnance Survey Landranger Map No.9.

Five-Degree West Challenge

One of the most challenging long-distance walks in Britain, this 'challenge' involves walking 220 miles up the five-degree west line of longitude from the Cowal Peninsula in the south to Cape Wrath in the north. By sticking as closely as possible to the line, the route has some serious obstacles to overcome, not least the 20,000-odd metres of ascent and a fair few rivers to ford. So if you've ever fancied yourself a bit of a Bear Grylls (and are, in fact, a dab foot at traversing tricky climbs, as this isn't one for the inexperienced), here's your chance to strut your stuff without being dropped from an aeroplane in Borneo.

For details see the Long Distance Walkers Association website at www.ldwa.org.uk

Other Long-Distance Walks

There are several other recognised long-distance walks across Scotland that are a little less hard-core. The Great Glen Way, linking Fort William and Inverness, travels up the side of Loch Ness (so don't forget your binoculars); while the Southern Upland Way is a coast-to-coast walk from Portpatrick in the west through the Borders to Cockburnspath in the east. And, in the spirit of cross-border peace and love there's St Cuthbert's Way, starting at Melrose and crossing the Eildon Hills on its way across the border to the Holy Island of Lindisfarne in England.

Details of all the walks can be found at http://walking.visitscotland.com

The A836

The what? That's right. The A836. More precisely, the A836 and the A838 and then the A894. In simple terms, the road that runs right across the northern coast of Scotland, from John O'Groats in the east to Durness in the west (a distance of around 93 miles) and then down the Sutherland Coast. Much of the road is single track and is cyclable, though you'll need Chris Hoy's thighs and a year's supply of energy bars. It's worth the struggle, though, to see the pristine but bare mountains and moorland to the south, as well as the succession of spectacular bays and inlets like the Kyle of Tongue and Loch Eriboll, to name a few.

Highland Wildcat Trails

If you're serious about mountain biking then it doesn't come much better than this. A series of linked trails, graded blue, red and black like ski runs, snakes its way through the forests above Golspie on the Dornoch Firth. Featuring the longest freeride descent in Britain, 400 metres from the summit of Ben Bhraggie, you'll also find the longest technical single-track climb. It's full-on stuff with big berms and drop-offs – and if you don't know what those are then you're better off staying at home.

Entrance to the park is by a £4 donation. www.scottishmountainbike.com

Munro Bagging

This activity, peculiar to Scotland, is known elsewhere as hill-walking. Munro baggers are the gladiators of the outdoor world – Gore-Tex-clad warriors whose foremost aim in life is to climb all 283 of Scotland's peaks that tower over 3000 feet (914.4 metres). Named after Sir Hugh Munro, who first catalogued Scotland's mountains in the 19th century, Munro bagging remains a significant challenge, particularly as one of the peaks in Skye's Cuillin Mountains forms a nerve-wracking rock spire. The best advice is to climb one of the easier Bens and call it a day. After all, a Munro in the bag's worth a pint in the pub.

www.themunrosociety.com

Malt Whisky Trail

If all that talk of walking makes you dizzy, here's an excuse for what Robert Burns called 'a cup o' kindness'. Such is the emotive power of the Scottish elixir that there's an official trail wriggling from distillery to distillery across Speyside, taking in a grand total of nine whisky-makeries, including seven of the region's most distinctive brands. There are some classics, like Chivas Regal and Glenfiddich, and some lesser-known malts from smaller distilleries that are every bit as good.

www.maltwhiskytrail.com

resipole farm

Where can you go camping if you fancy spending half your time ruining your body in the name of physical exertion, and the other half trying to improve your mind (well, the cultural part of it at least)? Is there a campsite whose philosophy embraces both fast and slow lanes? A campsite where you can do extreme exercise one day, then an art course the next? It surely can't exist, can it? But it does, here at Resipole Farm, out on the western edge of the Highlands next to the shining shores of Loch Sunart.

Knowing that Resipole is a place frequented by the outdoorsy active-types, we sent members of the *Cool Camping* (muddy) biking team to inspect the site, hoping to get their (mucky) single-track minds improved in the process, as nothing is said to be utterly impossible.

What they found was an unmistakable 'activity aura' enveloping the whole site, with canoes and sailing boats being hauled to and from the loch, mountain bikers returning from a long day in the saddle in wonderfully filthy states, as well as plenty of folk – the 'average family' campers, if you like – who only want to get out there sometimes, but are happy to spend the rest of their holidays exertion-free.

Although this is a big campsite, which gets pretty busy in midsummer, the effect as a whole (thanks to big pitches and careful landscaping) results in a pleasant environment that never feels too hectic, or full. If it does get full, though, and you show up on your bike or on foot, it's guaranteed that room will be found for you.

What really matters here, though, is not how big the pitches are, nor how superb the facilities, but what you can do to your body (and mind) in the world surrounding Resipole Farm. The boating potential has already been floated in paddle and wind mode, but there is also a slipway for launching small powered craft into Loch Sunart, which is big enough for everyone to take advantage of without bumping into one another's craft or flipper.

Of course, not everyone has aspirations to be the great iron man of the wilds, and for those whose concerns aren't as focused on all things outdoors, but love the look of the landscape, that matter of art and culture can be experienced here too. The campsite's cycle-friendly owners (bless 'em) run the Resipole Studios, which, despite seeming a bit out of place in this big, bad, wild, outdoor world, provide a hefty heap of culture to balance out all that adventure. Here campers can not only check out the various summer exhibitions and indulge their wallets on varying forms of art to stick on the walls back home, but they can even have a dabble at creating some artistic masterpieces of their own. Our biking team failed miserably at this, so we won't be exhibiting at the Tate this year, but you never know, one of you could be a budding Renoir or a much better Hockney.

But enough of that art malarkey, and back to the important matter of biking, because this area is about as good as it gets for rampant cyclists, with the quiet lochside road giving velocipedic access to rides as far as your legs will take you. Pedalling to the ruins of Castle Tioram makes a pleasant day out, Kentra Bay is amazing and Ardnamurchan Point – there and back – is about 55 miles of pleasure and pain. If it all proves too much (it is a lumpy landscape) the 'art' of knowing when you've had half enough could be handy. With Ben Resipole peeping up out of the scenery just behind the site, it ain't half bad for walkers here either. Or landscape painters, for that matter.

THE UPSIDE Splendid location on the edge of Loch Sunart, in an unspoilt, largely undiscovered corner of Scotland.
THE DOWNSIDE Despite the location, this is a big and sometimes busy site. (It can also be busy with midges.)
THE DAMAGE Tent and 2 adults £14. Additional adults £3 each; children £2. Tent and 2 cyclists/backpackers £12.
THE FACILITIES Modern and comprehensive amenities with showers, toilets, hot and cold washbasins, dishwashing, laundry, and disabled facilities. Electric hook-ups are available and there's an onsite shop selling the essentials.
NEAREST DECENT PUB The Salen Hotel (01967 431661; www.salenhotel.co.uk) is 2 miles away, and fortunately it's a pleasant place where decent food can be found. About 5 miles away, Ardshealach Lodge (01967 431399; www.ardshealach-lodge.co.uk) at Acharacle also has a good restaurant that offers 3-course evening meals from £20 per person.
IF IT RAINS Take either a stack of good books or your waterproofs (or both) or while away some time at the Resipole Studios.
GETTING THERE From the A82 Glasgow–Fort William road, 10 miles south of Fort William, cross Loch Linnhe by the Corran Ferry then follow the A861 for about 20 miles to the site.
PUBLIC TRANSPORT Bus no. S48 run by Shiel Buses (01967 431272) travels between Fort William and Kilchoan. The nearest stop to Resipole is Salen, a couple of miles away.
OPEN Apr–Oct.
IF IT'S FULL Ardnamurchan Campsite (p97), a further 20 miles westwards, is a very different kind of site, being small with basic facilities, but it has a glorious view and, again, is a cyclist's paradise.

Resipole Farm Holiday Park, Loch Sunart, Acharacle, Argyll PH36 4HX

| t | 01967 431235 | w | www.resipole.co.uk | 17 | on the map |

ardnamurchan

Campsites are usually quite easy to pigeonhole: busy, quiet, handy for town, quirky, friendly, run by Mr and Mrs Grumpy, good for cycling, great for walking, fantastic onsite massage parlour...Actually, forget the last one, that's another book entirely.

But the quality that we spend most of our time looking for is one that can't really be explained – because it's more of a feeling or experience – of simply being in a place that makes you feel good, giving off a vibe that everything is right with the world, even if it isn't. And this is what it feels like at Ardnamurchan Campsite. No matter how desperate things have become in the real world, there is a feeling here that it can't touch you. A McShangri-La by the sea if you like, an alternative world where crime, pollution, population problems and clubcard points are of no significance.

It could be that all this is just romanticised rubbish, of course, and that the simple thing that makes Ardnamurchan so special is that it is so wonderfully physically remote from real life – being the westernmost campsite in mainland Britain and reached only by a journey along the very worst strip of tarmac imaginable; really, it's terrible. So that by the time the campsite is gratefully in sight,

you're just thankful to find somewhere to pitch up and put your head down.

But Ardnamurchan turns out to be a combination of all that's best about camping: a very small site, in a spectacular location, offering stunning views over a loch. It also has that eccentric appearance that suggests a real person did all this for the love of it – not just to make a quick buck. We know this to be true because Trevor Potts, the man who created the campsite, did it all himself: it was he who single-handedly dug out the terraces; he who built the ablutional stuff with all the recycled materials he could find instead of just ordering it from Travis Perkins in Fort William. It was even he who built the replica of Shackleton's remarkable little boat that stands next to the campsite. There is nothing fancy or arty about what Trevor has done here, but he did it all himself, and everything fits in neatly with the surroundings. It feels like you're camping on a genuine working highland croft – which is what this site used to be.

So, what else does the Ardnamurchan Peninsula have to tempt campers? Well, some of the loveliest beaches on the planet can be found around the campsite's edges, as well as a remarkable remnant of a volcano

(unlike any other in Britain) nearby. The road to the beach at Sanna Bay goes right through the middle of the crater, so you can't help but abandon the car to walk around the rim of this real (but thankfully extinct) volcano. A fairly unique experience, it may just pique your interest in all things geological. The 18th-century croft has been converted into a study centre, equipped with all sorts of things from microscopes to mini exhibitions and even a couple of whale skeletons. Weekly lectures take place here over July and August, when you can also take part in fossil hunting or 'bugs and beasties' themed family walks around the area.

Ardnamurchan is a place of geographical wonder and scenic superlatives, but the blinding beaches and stunning views can't fully explain why this place grips your spirit so tightly and entices you to make the journey back. If we were to find a pigeonhole for this place, it would simply have to be the 'inexplicably special' one.

THE UPSIDE The view. The wildlife that can be spotted here (otters, pine martens, sea eagles and the stars of the show: golden eagles). The beaches all over Ardnamurchan Peninsula. The beautiful journey to get here (if you are the passenger), and that indefinable feeling of all-round salubriousness.
THE DOWNSIDE The tortuous journey to get here (if you are the driver) – and back. Waiting for the next opportunity to return.
THE DAMAGE Tent and 2 adults £12; children £3; family rate £16; backpacker £7. Dogs are free.
THE FACILITIES Basic and quaintly ramshackle, with toilets, showers, laundry, dishwashing facilities and electric hook-ups.

NEAREST DECENT PUB Kilchoan House Hotel (01972 510200; www.kilchoanhousehotel.co.uk) is 1½ miles away and provides bar meals or, when pre-booked, proper dining experiences. Guests are also encouraged to bring their own instruments along to create impromptu music in the public bar. So if you're a budding KT Tunstall or Jack Johnson pack that guitar alongside your tent.
IF IT RAINS Anyone for Scrabble? Or else a day out to Tobermory on the ferry (for timetable details see www.calmac.co.uk) makes a nice, genteel change from outdoor activities. Ardnamurchan Lighthouse (01972 510210) has a visitor centre and an extremely good café. But if it's not raining too hard, join Trevor on one of his guided walks or attend one of his lectures on local, as well as Antarctic, geology and wildlife.
GETTING THERE From the A82 take the ferry from Corran to Ardgour, the A861 for 25 miles to Salen, then a left on to the B8007. On reaching Kilchoan follow the lane along the coast, and the site is almost at the end of this.
PUBLIC TRANSPORT It is possible to get here by public transport (but one heck of an effort). Take a train to Oban, ferry to Mull, then bus to Tobermory, from where the ferry to Kilchoan sails. Then it's a further 3 mile-trek to the campsite.
OPEN Apr–Sept.
IF IT'S FULL The nearest site is at Resipole Farm (p93).

Ardnamurchan Campsite, Ormsaigbeg, Kilchoan, Acharacle PH36 4LL

| t | 01972 510766 or 07787 812084 | w | www.ardnamurchanstudycentre.co.uk | 18 | on the map |

the shielings

The Isle of Mull, despite being one of the most southerly and easiest to access of the Inner Hebridean islands, is surprisingly unspoilt and very little molested by the tourist industry. Just about all the visitors to the island arrive on the impressive Caledonian MacBrayne ship, the *MV Isle of Mull*, which sails from Oban to the island's ferry terminal at Craignure. That such numbers travel to and from this sleepy little bay is quite bizarre. The two-hourly drama can be watched from the site: for a few minutes the place is thick with folk, then when the ship disappears, the place is deserted again, and you wonder whether it was all just a dream.

The Shielings stands on the edge of the bay, overlooking not only the ferry terminal but also a colossal vista of glorious West Highland scenery taking in the Sound of Mull and Loch Linnhe, beyond which stand the highest hills in Britain. Besides having an extraordinary view, The Shielings is not just an ordinary campsite, as campers can have a choice of accommodation. Yes, you can bring your own tent and pitch it overlooking the view (or in a more sheltered position, if you like), but you can also choose from a variety of fixed 'shielings', which can be hired by the night or, more likely, by the week.

These shielings are, in effect, all-weather tents, and come equipped with beds, tables, chairs, a kitchen and even a heater. The posher models also have en suite bathrooms. For those without en suite ablutional arrangements, the site facilities are excellent, so there's no need to rough it here.

Should you eventually tire of the view and the comings and goings at the ferry terminal, you can't help but notice, or indeed hear, the Isle of Mull Steam Railway chuntering back and forth along the seaward edge of the site. The station is just 100 metres away, and from there a narrow-gauge train takes passengers just over a mile to Torosay Castle and Gardens. In early summer, the gardens are bright enough to hurt sensitive southern eyes, so remember to pack your shades. Another couple of scenic away-from-it-all miles on foot towards Duart Point reveal one of Scotland's classic sights, Duart Castle, which grows gradually more imposing as you approach. Back to Craignure, and if you've brought along a canoe or two, or even a boat, these can be launched at the front of the site where there's a handy slip road straight into the Sound of Mull.

Even though Mull is an island, you can get to the mainland quickly and cheaply using the Fishnish–Lochaline ferry five miles north of the Shielings; it can seem easier to reach than other places that are actually on the mainland, such as Morvern or Ardnamurchan, which are incredibly remote.

Bring your bikes to Mull for some serious traffic-free miles and a wilderness experience not found anywhere else in Britain. There's an excellent cycle ride to the island's main (and only) town at Tobermory, at the northern end of Mull. It's a 40-mile round trip, but taken over the whole day, and in decent weather, it isn't nearly as arduous as it is scenic. Tobermory is famous for being the inspiration and setting for the kids' TV show *Balamory*, but the island was famous before that for its wildlife, and especially its population of sea eagles. They can usually be seen around Loch Frisa, where there are organised eagle-spotting trips, but also at several other coastal areas on the island.

You don't need to be eagle-eyed to appreciate the spectacular beauty of this wee island, and the Shielings is the perfect base from which to explore it all.

THE UPSIDE Spectacular location, comfortable camping, easy access from the ferry.
THE DOWNSIDE Can get a little draughty.
THE DAMAGE Tent and 2 people £14/15 low/high season, extra adults £5, children £2.50, dogs £1; shielings £30/190 per night/week for 2 adults; en suite shielings £45/285 per night/week; hostel £12.50 per night.
THE FACILITIES Excellent amenities including free hot showers, toilets, washbasins, disabled facilities and laundry. 'Checklists' are provided free of charge so children can head out creature-spotting around the site, ticking off any of the various species of shell, flora and abundant wildlife they catch sight of in this natural haven. CDs and albums documenting the red deer, sea

otters, dolphins, porpoises and birds that visit the site are also available at reception, giving details on the best times to see them, along with a helpful map telling you where, too.
NEAREST DECENT PUB There are only a couple of pubs in the area and, thankfully, they're good ones. The Craignure Inn (01680 812305) 200 metres away has a varied menu and also does takeaway pizzas. MacGregor's Roadhouse (01680 812471) is also handy, with top-notch grub.
IF IT RAINS Torosay Castle and Gardens (01680 812421; www.torosay.com) are a 10-minute walk from the site, or get the ferry to Oban for a mosey around the town. The Scottish Sealife Sanctuary (01631 720386; www.sealsanctuary.co.uk) is about 10 miles away in Barcaldine and has an impressive

array of water-loving creatures, including sharks. The Isle of Mull Hotel (08709 506267) has a lovely swimming pool and spa facilities if you fancy treating yourself.
GETTING THERE From the ferry terminal at Craignure turn left (south) and the Shielings is 300 metres on the left, overlooking the bay.
PUBLIC TRANSPORT Take the train to Oban then hop on a ferry to Craignure.
OPEN Easter–Oct.
IF IT'S FULL There's Fidden Farm (p109) at the extreme south-west of the island, or much nearer is Balmeanach Campsite (01680 300342) at Fishnish, 5 miles north. Facilities here are also excellent, and the site is more sheltered, but consequently the midges are more problematic.

Shieling Holidays, Craignure, Isle of Mull PA65 6AY

| | t | 01680 812496 | w | www.shielingholidays.co.uk | 19 | on the map |

fidden farm

Fidden Farm isn't so much a campsite as a place to camp, and if there's nobody camping, which is quite common in the marginal months, then it is impossible to distinguish the place from any other stretch of deserted unspoilt coastline where the odd sheep is whiling away the day enjoying the view. There are no signs telling you that you've arrived at a campsite (no signs telling you anything, actually) and many a baffled camper must surely have turned around, disappointed, and left thinking that maybe there isn't a campsite here after all. But there is, and it's thriving – just in a very quiet way.

The drive to Fidden Farm from the ferry terminal at Craignure is just short of 40 miles, and besides being one of the loveliest 40 miles on the planet they are probably also some of the longest – as the road bucks and bobs its single-track way through, round, over and under a variety of scenery as diverse as any in Britain. It's worth a couple of nights camping at Fidden Farm just for the experience of the journey to get there, and back. Especially if your chosen means of motivation is a bike.

When scenery-stained campers eventually arrive at Fidden Farm, still reeling from the sights en route, what they stumble upon is almost as unexpected as it is enchanting. The site (but not a site) stands on several acres of close-cropped wind-blown turf that meanders along the coast in a series of small bays, enclosed by low, granite headlands with crystal-clear turquoise waters lapping over dazzling white-sand beaches. Once here, you'll find it is completely impossible not to stand and stare; so much so that managing to do anything that requires you to be inside your tent will be nothing short of miraculous.

All in all, it takes a good couple of days to calm down, let the mental metabolism adjust to 'Fidden Farm time' and come to terms with your good fortune in finding the place. Bring everything you have in the way of bikes and canoes, and be prepared to use them; the heavily indented coastline of Mull makes it perfect for sea kayaking, and the traffic-free roads are as biker friendly as they are joyously scenic.

Most of the time Fidden Farm is getting-away-from-it-all-camping in no uncertain terms, but apparently, for the first two weeks of the English school holidays, half the nation feels the urge to escape and a good proportion, it seems, migrate here, so do choose your time wisely.

So, what else is there to do besides canoeing, biking, bird-watching or just wandering about in a trance of slightly detached amazement? Surely that's enough? If not, the pilgrimage to the island of Iona can be made from Fionnphort either purely for sightseeing reasons or for a lovely stroll around the entire island (about 9 miles). Those with deeper religious intent may want to visit Iona Abbey, where Christianity first washed up on these beautiful shores. And while you're prowling around Fionnphort, waiting for a ferry, the café and shop can be inspected too. The shop stocks everything you're likely to need, including the famously delicious Selkirk Bannock Bun, a rich fruit bun that is all anybody really needs in life. Also accessible from Fionnphort is the small, uninhabited island of Staffa, which resembles the Giant's Causeway in Northern Ireland. And that's it – anything else is miles (and miles) away, but then surely that's the whole point of getting away from it all.

THE UPSIDE Far, far from the madding crowd, and in an incredibly beautiful location.
THE DOWNSIDE Life can get a bit breezy here.
THE DAMAGE £6 per adult per night, £3 per child per night.
THE FACILITIES A new, well-equipped modern toilet block includes 2 men's, 2 women's, and 1 disabled user's toilet as well as hot showers and washing-up sink. There is also a water tap next to the farm.
NEAREST DECENT PUB There is only

one, and thankfully the Keel Row Restaurant (01681 700458) is a cracker, only a mile or so from the site, it offers excellent traditional food (served between 6 and 8:30pm, so get there early) and beers.
IF IT RAINS Take a few good books or be prepared to get wet canoeing, walking or cycling.
GETTING THERE Take the A849 from the ferry terminal at Craignure signposted to Fionnphort and Iona then, in the centre of Fionnphort, turn left into the lane to Fidden Farm.

PUBLIC TRANSPORT Bowmans Coaches (01680 812313) runs bus no. 496 from Craignure ferry terminal to Fionnphort.
OPEN Easter–Oct.
IF IT'S FULL There is another *Cool Camping* site on the Isle of Mull at the Shielings (p105), though this is of a very different nature. If getting-away-from-it-all is the order of the day then consider the 'official' wild camping place at Calgary Bay (on the north-western shore of the island).

Fidden Farm Campsite, Knockvologan Road, Nr Fionnphort, Isle of Mull PA66 6BN		
	t 01681 700427	20 on the map

invercaimbe

There are numerous ways to describe a sunset: you can eulogise its fiery reds, deep oranges, the images of melting flames hitting the ocean, all the usual clichés and hyperbole. There is a sunset in Scotland, though, that may just manage to defy words.

At Invercaimbe you can take a ringside seat on the beach by the campsite and watch the drama as the sun enjoys its dalliance with the Atlantic over the Small Isles of Rum, Eigg and Muck in a setting bathed in a similarly deep glow of history.

This corner of the world possesses a real sense of the epic, the perfect backdrop for one of the most colourful periods in Scottish history, the '45 Jacobite rebellion whose mere mention still mists the eyes of many a Highlander. The unlikely and more than a little effete figure of Bonnie Prince Charlie landed at Glenfinnan in 1745 in an attempt to enlist the Highlanders in an audacious bid to reclaim his right to the British throne. After a shaky start and some understandable reluctance the clans massed and spent the ensuing months notching up victories as they built momentum on the charge south, reaching as far as Derby and spiralling London into a panic.

The failure of the rebellion – the Jacobites eventually retreated north and were brutally massacred on the moor of Culloden a year later – led to the complete breakdown of life as the Highlanders knew it. The British government banned the wearing of kilts, the playing of bagpipes and the clan system that had formed the backbone of Highland life for centuries. Its direct and indirect effects can still be felt in what is one of the EU's poorest regions today, adding a shade of pathos to the grandiose scenery as you stand on the beach that lies right in front of a campsite and enjoys a prime position on the sandy dunes overlooking the Atlantic.

The Invercaimbe Caravan and Campsite, which has only 20 pitches, lies right at the heart of Bonnie Prince Charlie country and makes a great base for exploring the legacy. You can visit Borrodale where the 'Young Pretender' first set foot on the mainland with only a handful of men – rather than the promised 10,000 Frenchmen – and then head south to the visitor centre at Glenfinnan to see a recreation of the day when the skirl of the pipes echoed around one of Scotland's most scenic glens for that last fateful massing of the clans, before returning to Loch nan Uamh where he fled on a French frigate a year later, less than a mile from where his escapade began.

Once you have followed the history trail, Invercaimbe itself awaits with its simple pleasures. The wide sandy beach and sheltered sea inlet on two sides are perfect for paddling and swimming; you can also hire out kayaks and canoes at Ach na skia (www.achnaskiacroft.co.uk) next door. This is the sort of place where you tend to just lose a day or two not doing very much,

without even realising. When the weather is glorious, there is no better place to be and when it is not, it just adds to the drama.

The highlight at Invercaimbe is, of course, one of those sharp-intake-of-breath inducing sunsets. There is little point in trying to describe it; for a real picture you will fortunately need to come here for yourself. Suffice to say that Invercaimbe's sunsets provide a fitting backdrop for departing princes and tragic lost causes.

THE UPSIDE Epic drama from sunsets to bonnie princes.
THE DOWNSIDE A lifetime wasted trying to find comparable sunsets afterwards.
THE DAMAGE £10 for a 2-person tent.
THE FACILITIES Toilets, showers, laundry, dishwashing room. There are 16 electric hook-ups.
NEAREST DECENT PUB Whether you eat in the bar or the restaurant of the Arisaig Hotel (01687 450210) you will find a medley of fresh seafood. The creamy East Coast Cullen Skink and dish of Loch-Nan-Uamh mussels are both first class.

Cnoc-na-Faire (01687 450249) at the top of the hill is a stylish alternative, offering cracking views and gourmet breakfasts.
IF IT RAINS Head south to the visitor centre at Glenfinnan Monument (01397 722250) to follow in the prince's footsteps. You can also join West Coast Railway's famous steam-train journey – 'The Jacobite' – that runs from March to October. Travelling from Mallaig down to Fort William, it takes in a staggering amount of spectacular scenery and was voted by *Wanderlust* magazine in 2009 as the 'Top Railway Journey in the World'.

The Ardnamurchan Lighthouse (01972 510210) is also worth a tour.
GETTING THERE Take the A830 from Fort William through Glenfinnan towards Mallaig. After you pass through Arisaig look out for the signposts to Invercaimbe.
PUBLIC TRANSPORT The Shiel Bus (01967 431272) service between Fort William and Mallaig passes the campsite on the A830.
OPEN Easter–Oct.
IF IT'S FULL Another *Cool Camping* site in the area is Camusdarach (p119), 3 miles north of here.

Invercaimbe Caravan and Campsite, Arisaig, Inverness-shire PH39 4NT

| | t | 01687 450375 | w | www.invercaimbecaravansite.co.uk | 21 | on the map |

camusdarach

Camusdarach must surely be one of Britain's best all-round holiday destinations, but before getting into all the usual stuff, perhaps an explanation of the philosophy behind the running of the place may partially explain why a simple campsite can feel so thoroughly salubrious, and why everybody seems so relaxed and friendly while camping at Camusdarach.

The Simpsons (Andrew and Angela), from the Thames Valley, arrived in this little corner of coastal paradise some 15 years ago with a vision to turn a dilapidated farm and campsite into something special. But, because this is such a special place in the natural sense, they decided that everything would need to be eco-driven and completely sustainable to retain this natural beauty. And they succeeded – it is extremely special.

Most of the day-to-day landscape management is done by a small flock of endangered Hebridean sheep, while the trendy and very plush toilet block (renewable softwood) releases effluents into gravel beds and wetlands planted with specific plants whose job it is to detoxify the environment they grow in. There has been no artificial landscaping of the two camping fields, because none is needed, and this whole philosophy of respecting nature

and doing everything possible to fit in with it shines through to the everyday outlook of the running of the site. It's informal and friendly, and campers are treated as intelligent individuals, all of which is partly responsible for that indefinable feeling of wellbeing. In turn, everybody respects their neighbours and the site.

However, no matter how well run or eco-friendly a campsite may be, it is only really as good as the opportunities around it, and Camusdarach is engulfed by them. First and foremost are the seaside scenes that the site nestles among, with miles of dunes giving way to blindingly white sandy beaches. You can walk for miles along the strands here, never really coming to terms with the fact that this really is north-western Scotland, and not the Caribbean. The islands of Skye, Rum, Eigg, Canna and Muck punctuate the horizon across the azure waters, and you just can't help but feel good in this vision of paradise. Memories of places like this sustain us through the long winters.

Many come here for a week and never move a motorised wheel for the whole duration, such is the basic appeal of the immediate surroundings, but another 'however' is due here, for the natural beauty of this area isn't restricted to this glorious seaside fringe.

Visitors should turn their eyes inland to the lochs and hills for further inspiration, firstly towards Loch Morar, the deepest sheet of freshwater in Britain. Loch Morar is easy and rewarding to explore, be it on foot, partly by bike (from the site then on foot) or, better still, by canoe.

The road that leads to Camusdarach ends six miles further along at the small fishing port of Mallaig, which feels like a frontier town. It has the fascination of a real place (with shops if you need them), warts and all, and a place gripped by the constant comings and goings of a variety of sea-faring vessels. The big ferry to Skye is one such coming and going, while the supply ship to the Small Isles (Rum, Muck, Eigg and Canna) makes a daily trip through amazing scenery.

From this superb little campsite, set in seaside heaven, you can stumble out every day and gasp incredulously for weeks if the weather plays at all fair. And it often does here. There's nothing more to say and nothing more to write, as coming here is the only way to truly understand the feeling that this place provokes.

THE UPSIDE Everything – the site, the location, the surroundings.
THE DOWNSIDE Having to leave.
THE DAMAGE £16 for a tent and occupants on a serviced pitch.
THE FACILITIES Superb modern eco-block containing free showers, toilets, washbasins, disabled facilities, baby-changing, dishwashing and laundry. A mobile shop visits twice weekly.
NEAREST DECENT PUB The nearest is the Morar Hotel (01687 462346), which has a public bar equipped with a great selection of malt whiskies, and the Silver Sands restaurant has a stunning view out over the beaches of Morar.

Food is mainly traditional with salmon, trout, and venison on offer. The Cnoc-na-Faire Hotel (01687 450249) at Arisaig is highly recommended for its good food, while there is also a Thai takeaway (01687 462259) in Morar.
IF IT RAINS Boat trips from Mallaig can be taken to the Isle of Skye on the ferry, or to Knoydart and Loch Nevis on the little boat (01687 462320) that carries supplies and mail to the outlying farms with no road access. The journey to Fort William from Mallaig by train is a memorable one, giving an armchair view of big scenery en route.
GETTING THERE From the A830 Fort William–Mallaig road take the B8008 through Arisaig and along the coast. The site is on the left about 4 miles north of Arisaig.
PUBLIC TRANSPORT Head to Fort William where Shiel Buses (01967 431272) operate a service to Mallaig that stops at Arisaig's post office. It's a hefty walk from there, though, so it's best to book a taxi while en route. Camusdarach's website (see below) has a comprehensive list of alternative options, including helicopter charters if you really want to arrive in style.
OPEN Mar–Oct.
IF IT'S FULL Another Cool Camping site in the area is Invercaimbe (p115) 3 miles to the south of Camusdarach.

Camusdarach, Arisaig, Inverness-shire PH39 4NT

| | t | 01687 450221 | w | www.camusdarach.com | 22 | on the map |

faichemard farm

Imagine the scene. You arrive after a long journey at a gorgeous campsite and pitch in a secluded spot where the only sounds are the birds singing and the gentle breeze rustling through the trees. You skip off to the local pub and, a few pints and a hearty dinner later, return full of the joys of camping. But cue the arrival of a frantic family of seven with a four-room mega-tent and a generator capable of powering a small town and the bucolic calm you've been savouring is shattered. The sounds of nature are replaced by incessant all-night kid-screaming and the thud of footballs bouncing off your tent.

Mercifully, at Faichemard Farm, this is an experience guaranteed not to happen, as this is one of the very few adults-only campsites in Scotland. The added bonus is a sweeping mountain backdrop and a location surrounded by forests.

At the end of Faichemard's first adults-only season (2006), owner Duncan Grant admitted that he had been overwhelmed by the response: 'We thought there might be a wee gap in the market, but nothing like this, with enquiries and campers pouring in from all over Scotland and from further afield too'. In addition to the ban on children, neither ball games nor cycling are allowed, though this is in no way a reflection of an unfriendly site, more indicative of it being a retreat for like-minded people looking for a quieter camping experience.

With only 35 pitches spread across an expansive 10-acre forest site, there is no danger of overcrowding, and even in high season Duncan is not tempted to squeeze in any more. The main, flat area is set around a small pond and is where most people congregate in summer when, on calm overcast days, the infamous Highland midge is out in force on the rest of the site.

On sunny and breezy days, when midge activity is greatly reduced, the hillside pitches tempt with the chance to camp among the fragrant heather and enjoy your own private Highland retreat. Each pitch also has its own picnic table where you can sit and munch away or enjoy a Highland sundowner with the Glengarry Mountains in the background.

With the adults-only policy and the site's enviable position among the hills and mountains, it is no surprise that Faichemard Farm is popular with walkers and climbers. Within easy striking distance is Ben Tee, whose 901-metre high mass can easily be seen from the campsite, as well as the more challenging mountains of Kintail.

The campsite also attracts walkers trekking the Great Glen Way (see Walks and Wheel Trails, p89), the most northerly of Scotland's two coast-to-coast walks, which cuts north-east from the railhead at Fort William in search of lochs Linnhe, Lochy, Oich and Ness, culminating at Inverness.

Cycling may be banned at the site itself, but Faichemard Farm makes a good base for cycling on the Great Glen Way and for the world-famous mountain-biking tracks in the Nevis Range. But whether you spend the day powering up to the dizzy heights of a Munro, cycling around Loch Ness or simply relaxing at the local pub, Faichemard Farm makes the perfect, quiet, kid-free retreat. The only unexpected noise may be the occasional sound of Duncan Grant coaxing a few tunes out of his trusty bagpipes, a sign that although this place is adults-only, it still manages to retain a sense of fun.

THE UPSIDE An adults-only campsite that offers an oasis of calm.

THE DOWNSIDE The midges are a problem among the trees and bushes; stick to the main campsite on overcast summer days.

THE DAMAGE £12 per 2-person tent then £3.50 per extra adult. Electricity is £1.50. Dogs are welcome but must be kept on leads.

THE FACILITIES There are 2 toilet blocks with hot showers as well as shaver points, a washing machine and a tumble-dryer.

NEAREST DECENT PUB The Invergarry Hotel (01809 501206) offers reasonable pub grub and a good selection of ales. It lies within walking distance and has cosy log fires to boot.

IF IT RAINS Learn more about the region's infrastructure at the Caledonian Canal Heritage Centre (01320 366493) and the Clansman Centre (01320 366444), which are both in nearby Fort Augustus.

GETTING THERE From Inverness take the A82 along the north bank of Loch Ness. Turn right on to the A87 at Invergarry (signposted for Kyle of Lochalsh) and continue through the village for a mile. Turn right on to a minor road signposted 'Faichemard' and turn right at the 'A & D Grant, Faichemard Farm' sign.

PUBLIC TRANSPORT Citylink buses (08705 505050) running between Inverness and Fort William stop at Invergarry. The service is fairly infrequent, though, so it's advisable to call beforehand to check times.

OPEN Apr–Oct.

IF IT'S FULL Unfortunately, most of the sites around Loch Ness, to the north, are exclusively for caravans nowadays. Heading south, Linnhe Lochside Holidays (01397 772376; www.linnhe-lochside-holidays.co.uk) has a dedicated tent field among its lodges and statics, and a few waterside pitches.

Faichemard Farm Camping Site, Invergarry, Inverness-shire PH35 4HG

| | t | 01809 501314 | w | www.faichemard-caravancamping.co.uk | 23 | on the map |

rothiemurchus

If you like trees – seriously like trees – then Rothiemurchus campsite is the type of spot you might go to and never want to come back from. It's one of the best places in Scotland to enjoy swathes of indigenous Caledonian woodland, with a flurry of Scots pine, birch and juniper forests and wood-shrouded lochs. There is a real sense of being somewhere genuinely unspoilt and pristine here: clear evidence of how the land was formed during the last Ice Age 10,000 years ago and time-worn trees that will make you feel seriously mortal.

The award-winning campsite is set within the boundaries of the Rothiemurchus Estate, which itself lies right on the edge of the remarkable Cairngorm Mountain massif, the vast mountain plateau that was recently designated the UK's largest national park. There are caravans and static homes on the site, but trees quickly conceal these to leave you adrift in your own Forest of Eden.

You can choose from the main pitches, where you will see other tents and be close to the amenities, or you can head across one of the burns that rumble through the camp, the largest of which is the Am Beanaidh. It is a sublime experience waking up on a bed of soft needles on a summer morning to the sound of rushing water with the smell of pine spiking the crisp air.

People have been attracted to this woodland area since at least the Bronze Age. By the late 1500s, the land had fallen under the control of John Grant of Freuchie who bestowed it upon his second son, Patrick, the first Grant laird of Rothiemurchus. The Grant family has held the stewardship of the estate for over 400 years to the present day and its members have proved enlightened landowners, opening up the land for walkers, cyclists and tree lovers. Scotland's lingering feudal land ownership attracts its share of controversy, but Rothiemurchus is the type of inclusive estate that the Land Reform Act of 2003 was designed to encourage.

You can hire bikes from the visitor centre on the estate and meander around the myriad paths, with an easy circular route taking in the twin lochs of Morlich and Loch an Eilein. The latter is one of the prettiest in the country with a ruined castle sitting in the middle of the water and beaches fringing its edges. There are some more serious routes up past the outdoor activity centre at Glenmore that stretch into the mountains on old drovers' trails opening up remote lochs and isolated bothies.

Glenmore Lodge (01479 861256; www.glenmorelodge.org.uk) is a serious outdoor activity centre with a particular emphasis on climbing and mountaineering, being handy for the Cairngorms and some of Britain's finest ice-climbing, as well as plenty of summer routes. Novices can either seek advice from the centre or enrol on one of its frequently run courses.

If that's all a bit too adventurous, just climb aboard the Cairngorm Mountain Railway, the funky funicular railroad that eases up the mountainside revealing stupendous views with minimal effort. Be aware, though, that walkers cannot use the funicular and, equally, that funicular users cannot push on up to the summit.

Rothiemurchus is the sort of site that ticks so many different boxes. Forest camping at its finest, it works for those looking to get away from it all, those wanting to let loose on a bike or those who fancy a walk off into the challenging Cairngorm Mountains. And did we mention all the beautiful trees?

THE UPSIDE Trees, trees and more trees. Think of all those wonderful endorphins they will pump through your system.

THE DOWNSIDE The caravan site and static homes as you come in are a bit off-putting but you forget them once you're in among the trees.

THE DAMAGE £7 per adult per night and £2 for kids aged 5–16. In July and August adults are £8 per night, kids still £2.

THE FACILITIES There's a keycard-operated shower block with hot showers and toilets, all kept pristine.

NEAREST DECENT PUB The Old Bridge Inn (01479 811137) is only 2 miles away on the road to Aviemore. This atmospheric old inn, with a fine log fire, specialises in local dishes such as peppered leg of venison, with plenty of whiskies and real ales on hand to wash it down. Mains are £12–16, though, so eating's not cheap.

IF IT RAINS Rothiemurchus Estate lies just outside the resort town of Aviemore, the self-styled 'Adventure Capital of the Highlands', with its numerous amenities. The Macdonald Highland Resort (www.aviemorehighlandresort. com) is a fully equipped resort with swimming pools and restaurants.

GETTING THERE Rothiemurchus campsite is just a couple of miles off the A9. Coming north take the first turning for Aviemore and then follow the signs for Rothiemurchus. The site is visible after a couple of miles on the right-hand side.

PUBLIC TRANSPORT Regular bus services run from Aviemore to the Cairngorm Mountain Railway, passing the campsite on the way. Call Traveline (08712 002233) for timetables.

OPEN All year.

IF IT'S FULL The Cool Camping site at the Lazy Duck (p131) is nearby, but only has room for a few tents at a time. Otherwise try the Alvie & Dalraddy Estates site (01479 810330; www.alvie-estate.co.uk) 4 miles south of Aviemore off the A9.

Rothiemurchus Camp and Caravan Park, Rothiemurchus Estate, By Aviemore, Inverness-shire PH22 1QH

| | t | 01479 812800 | w | www.rothiemurchus.net/Pages/Activities/Camp-and-Caravan.html | 24 | on the map |

lazy duck

It says everything about the Lazy Duck that the resident half-dozen Aylesbury ducks are too lazy to even bother hatching their own young. Not for them, toiling to keep their eggs warm and then the hassle of having to rear the fluffy hatchlings. Oh no, they are far too busy relaxing around the lush pond, sunning themselves among the heather or seeking shade under the protective shelter of the giant Scots pines that rise all around.

The Lazy Duck seems to have a similarly soporific effect on campers too. It may be less than a mile from the nearest village at Nethy Bridge, but the rough single-track road takes you into another world, one where the towering massif of the Cairngorms dominates the background and the foreground opens up with the relaxing sounds of gently twittering birds and sights of swaying hammocks and rope swings.

The campsite was added in 2002 to a location that is still best known for the excellent Lazy Duck Hostel, which has been much eulogised in various guidebooks and is legendary among walkers and even the odd honeymooning couple. The campsite is very small indeed and booking is essential, with space for only four pitches, though the charming couple behind the Lazy Duck, David and Valery Dean, keep a spare spot

reserved only for those who come here on foot or by bike. The tents nestle in a small glade surrounded by trees. There is a rope swing, a hammock where you can idle away a few hours and a picnic bench, which comes complete with a chimenea to keep you warm on chillier evenings. The 'bush shower' provides a defiant stand against the British climate. Introduced by the Deans' son, who got the idea while working in Africa, it's an outdoor shower for which you carry a bucket of hot water from the hostel.

The two most popular spots at the Lazy Duck are the 'heather hammock' and the sauna. The former is a simple hammock stretched out between two trees in an idyllic spot away from the hostel and campsite. The views are sublime, with the heather moorland and patches of Caledonian forest stretching out in front, while the peaks of the Cairngorms, now protected as a national park, lurk to the rear. The sauna is not just an afterthought either, with a small chill-out area by the sauna room where you can light a candle, burn a little essential oil and listen to any of the collection of ambient CDs.

If you manage to rouse yourself from this wanton relaxation – no mean task here – then even setting out on a walk requires little effort, as the Speyside Way, one of

Scotland's designated network of marked long-distance trails, passes nearby. The area is also very popular with mountain bikers and you can cycle on the Speyside Way itself, around the Abernethy Forest or the Rothiemurchus Estate. The forest and estate are both highly regarded, with a variety of terrains from smooth forest roads to tough muddy single tracks through the thick trees. In winter there are ski slopes nearby; the Deans advise people to bring their own toboggan if they fancy a spot of sledging.

Back at the campsite, one of the simple pleasures is just watching the eponymous ducks amble through their day. They are joined in the ponds and Fhuarain Burn by myriad other birdlife including mandarin, wigeon, pintail and whileling duck, and the odd capercaillie can be spotted within the surrounding forest. They may not exactly qualify as ideal parents, but the Lazy Ducks may have a thing or two to teach stressed-out visiting campers with their relaxed approach to life.

THE UPSIDE The perfect place to get lazy.
THE DOWNSIDE There's a size limit; if your tent is big enough to accommodate more than 3 people it's too big. There are few pitches and you need to re-pitch on fresh grass after 3 nights.
THE DAMAGE £9 for a tent with 1 person, then £4 per extra person. Dogs aren't permitted.
THE FACILITIES Hot and cold water, washing-up space, a robust 'bush shower' all the way from 'down under' that's proving hugely popular with campers, sauna, wet-weather cooking shelter with seating for 10; free-range eggs when available plus veggies and bags of salad. A communal area with a chimenea. Long swing.

NEAREST DECENT PUB The Nethybridge Hotel (01479 821203) is within easy walking distance of the campsite; as is the Mount View Hotel (01479 821248), which specialises in posh nosh; or a 10-minute drive away, in Boat of Garten, Anderson's Restaurant (01479 831466) serves up good food including Highland lamb cooked to perfection.
IF IT RAINS The MacDonald Highland Resort (01479 815100; www.aviemorehighlandresort.com) in Aviemore is a great wet-weather base as you can stay there and use their swimming pool, eateries and also organise a variety of sports and day trips from there.

GETTING THERE From Aviemore take the A95 east and turn on to the unclassified road to the right, signposted for Nethy Bridge. Then turn left on to the B970, and right on to another unclassified road to enter Nethy Bridge. The campsite is on the edge of the village right off the Tomintoul road.
PUBLIC TRANSPORT Highland Country Buses (01479 811211) run services to Nethy Bridge from Aviemore and Grantown-on-Spey.
OPEN Apr–Oct (depending on ground conditions, so please email ahead).
IF IT'S FULL You can also stay at the Lazy Duck Hostel onsite, one of Scotland's best.

Lazy Duck Campsite, Nethy Bridge, Inverness-shire PH25 3ED

| | e | lazyduckhostel@googlemail.com | w | www.lazyduck.co.uk | 25 on the map |

ythan valley

Is there any part of Britain still unknown and undiscovered? Anywhere still anxiously awaiting (or dreading) a visit from its first tourist? Alas, probably not. But there are still a precious few hidden corners and secluded valleys in Scotland, free from any accommodation for the curious traveller. Ythan Valley was one such place, until Dave, Libby and daughter Iona decided to open a campsite in their garden-cum-meadow.

Despite it's rather Welsh-sounding name, Ythan Valley campsite really is Scottish, and can be found tucked away in a north-eastern corner of Aberdeenshire. This undisturbed part of Scotland can't compete with the Highlands for dramatic scenery, and thus there are fewer tourists. Those who do venture here tend to hug the coastal margins rather than stray inland where, in places such as Ythan Valley, visitors are usually limited to day-trippers.

But things have started to change since these five pitches at Smithfield Croft appeared, along with four beds in the onsite lodge. The campsite is tucked behind the croft on the edge of the small hamlet of Ythanbank, and from here the lucky and exclusively small number of campers can wander as lonely as clouds in the empty – but not bleak – surroundings.

Camping here is a comfortable experience indeed, and the welcome extraordinarily warm and friendly. You get the impression that the campsite staff (Libby and Iona) are really, at heart, doing this for the fun of it and to share their rural backwater with new folk. All the usual boring stuff like toilets and showers are available, but there's also the luxury of a campers' 'snug' in the old stone 'neep' shed, which has a touch of the Bedouin boudoir about it.

But that isn't all they do here to make you feel at home, for Libby and Iona (if school's out) do B&B, but not in the traditional sense; here it's 'bread and breakfast'. The early morning sustenance they rustle up is varied and delicious and can even be delivered to your tent if you so wish: full Scottish or veggie breakfasts, bacon butties, eggs-however and the speciality of the house – toast – or, more accurately, Libby's toasted freshly baked bread.

Campers can order a fresh loaf every day in a bewildering variety of seed mixtures and flavours including granary; pumpkin; sunflower; chickpea; coriander and cumin; cinnamon and raisin; onion and rosemary or just a plain white or brown loaf. You can even invent your own recipe. So be sure to ditch the diet before you come here.

All this talk of being in the back of beyond, while it feels true enough on the spot, may not be wholly accurate. For instance, if 'one' has a weakness for stately homes, Haddo House and Fyvie Castle are an easy drive or cycle away. Both boast landscaped gardens and rambling country parks with woodland and lakeside walks. All the better if you can strap a pair of tennis racquets to your handlebars, as there's also a tennis court at Haddo so you can further work off all that baked breakfast goodness.

The nearest settlement, Ellon, is four miles away and if campers still feel the need for the big city, the local urban madhouse that is Aberdeen lies just 25 miles away. This may seem like a long way in England, but up here, in the wider world, it's positively local.

But with the welcome, space, tranquillity and completely unspoilt nature of the countryside on hand at Ythan Valley, it's tempting to just stay put and maybe tuck into a little more of that bread.

THE UPSIDE The welcome, the bread, the slightly theatrical campers' lounge, the roaming ducks and the beautiful rambling surroundings.
THE DOWNSIDE Expanding waistlines; and it's a long way from anywhere.
THE DAMAGE Tent and 1 adult £8 per night; additional adults £4; children £2. The lodge costs from £15 per person per night.
THE FACILITIES Good facilities within the main building with toilet, shower, and dishwashing sink. Campers' snug in the old barn.
NEAREST DECENT PUB The Tolbooth (01358 721308) in Ellon is a traditional pub with a big selection of malt whiskies and no food to distract from the fine Scotch flavours. The Redgarth (01651 872353; www.redgarth.com) at Oldmeldrum has been CAMRA's Regional Pub of the Year numerous times, and serves good food; it's very popular with locals and campers alike.
IF IT RAINS Plenty of options: Haddo House (08444 932179) has gardens, a country park, and produce shop; Aberdeen Maritime Museum (01224 337700); Satrosphere Science Centre (01224 640340; www.satrosphere.net); Glen Garioch Distillery (01651 873450) does tours Mon–Sat; Codonas Amusement Park (01224 595910; www.codonas.com) is a standard theme park on the beach at Aberdeen. Then Dunnottar Castle (01569 762173; www.dunnottarcastle. co.uk) is one of the most impressive sights on the Scottish coast.
GETTING THERE Follow the A90 north from Aberdeen for 15 miles, then left on to the B9005 through Ellon. Continue along the road (including a right turn) to Ythanbank, and go straight on where the main road turns left, right into the first narrow lane, and right into Smithfield.
PUBLIC TRANSPORT There's a regular bus service from Aberdeen to Ellon, from where there's an infrequent bus service to Ythanbank. Check times with Traveline (08712 002233; www.traveline.org.uk).
OPEN All year.
IF IT'S FULL Nowhere within easy reach, so definitely book in advance.

Ythan Valley Campsite, Smithfield, Ythanbank, Nr Ellon, Aberdeenshire AB41 7TH

| t | 01358 761400 | 26 on the map |

hidden glen

No two campsites are ever completely alike, but we are fairly confident that the campsite at Hidden Glen has an authentic claim to being oddly unique in Britain. Not weird, or good, or bad, just unique.

There are a couple of reasons why this place tops the unique bill. The first matter is one of exclusivity, for camping here is a very exclusive affair, limited to just a few pitches, and only by prior arrangement with owners Peter and Therese, who have, in the past, been known to decide that a lone camper is sufficient for their purposes.

That may sound slightly sinister, but rest assured all that campers have been required to do here is, in effect, sing for their supper. Not literally sing of course, there's no danger of Simon Cowell springing out from behind a nearby bush to make you warble your way through a rendition of 'I Will Always Love You' before letting you pitch your tent. Thank goodness. The simple arrangement at Hidden Glen is that campers dedicate just an hour of their time working on the farm each day in exchange for the use of the campsite. It had only really been advertised in Holland and Germany before, but worked out so well with the European campers that the doors are now wide open to any hard-working Brits keen to join the fun at this campsite.

And what a campsite it is too. Lying on a gentle slope overlooking some vast and empty lands of afforested rolling hills that romp off relentlessly into the distance, the ground is home to the stony remnants of an Iron-Age hut village. And the principal pitch (because so far rarely no more than a single tent has been allowed at any given time) is sheltered within a ring of rocks and trees. This camping circle also houses a kitchen shelter (with grass roof), cooker and, round the back, a very Heath-Robinson-looking compost toilet. If you need a shower there is a bucket and plenty of privacy. Firewood is also provided for the built-in fireplace, plus a picnic bench for meal times. All in all it's a strange and hypnotic mix of the civilised and the wild all rolled into one very mysterious setting.

This may sound a little far fetched, but at night, safe in that stone circle, with the light from the fire dancing across the shadows, you can almost hear the wolves and bears that would have been present when man first camped in this exact spot in bygone years. Such is the elemental feel of this ancient place.

Back to working matters: this is quite a small farm and, in the past when work was scarce, Peter and Therese would match the camping numbers to the work quota. The

result was that this unspoilt, atmospheric place lying in the foothills of the northern Cairngorms, just four miles from the sea, could often be devoid of campers. What a waste, they thought, so decided to approach things in a slightly more flexible way.

They do still intend to allow campers the opportunity to 'toil in the soil' in exchange for camping fees, but when the workforce outstrips the need, surplus campers are required to pay a small camping fee.

The farm itself is devoted to a system of sustainable agriculture, complementing the surrounding wildlife rather than restricting it, and Therese grows an astounding array of organic vegetables. These, and the farm's free-range eggs are available to campers.

So what will it be? Toil in the soil, or dish the dosh? It doesn't matter either way really, as the highlight here is the circle of stones that transports you back to a time when living meant camping.

THE UPSIDE Remarkable setting among the ancient stone hut circles with the opportunity to pay for your pitch with your own labour.
THE DOWNSIDE No casual camping callers, and the facilities may take getting used to.
THE DAMAGE An hour's labour a day for each camper, or about £8 for a tent and 2 adults if there are more workers than work.
THE FACILITIES Grass-roofed shelter with compost toilet, water, cooker, cooking utensils and firewood. Just a bucket for a shower.
NEAREST DECENT PUB The nearest pubs are all in Nairn about 4 miles away and include the following: Havelock House (01667 455500) is only open during the day, but serves a nice lunch in its coffee shop and bistro; posh nosh can be found at the Classroom (01667 455999); or a mixture of good food and nice surroundings is on offer at the Cawdor Tavern (01667 404777) next to Cawdor Castle.
IF IT RAINS Get wetter still by rafting or canoeing in the nearby River Findhorn with the following: Ace Adventures (01479 810510; www.aceadventures.co.uk); Full On Adventure (07885 835838; www.fullonadventure.co.uk); Splash White Water Rafting (01887 829706; www.rafting.co.uk). Or visit Cawdor Castle (01667 404401; www.cawdorcastle.com) allegedly once home to one of Shakespeare's most blood-soaked villains, Macbeth. Benromach Distillery (01309 675968) at Forres and Dallas Dhu Distillery (01309 676548) both do tours.
GETTING THERE Follow the A939 south from Nairn towards Grantown-on-Spey for 3.5 miles, then turn left on to a track, following the sign for Laikenbuie Holidays.
PUBLIC TRANSPORT Take a train or bus to Nairn, then hop in a taxi.
OPEN All year.
IF IT'S FULL This is a unique experience, so do book in advance or stay in one of the lodges here. The Old Mill Caravan Park (01309 641244) near Forres is another option, though.

Hidden Glen Campsite, Laikenbuie Holidays, Grantown Road, Nairn, Inverness-shire IV12 5QN

| | t | 01667 454630 | w | www.hiddenglen.co.uk | 27 | on the map |

shiel bridge

Shiel Bridge is a legendary place among mountaineers, and anybody with aspirations to stand astride the most handsome mountains in Scotland will eventually find themselves in Glen Shiel, staring up at the famous Five Sisters of Kintail or contemplating the steep and slightly perilous ascent of the mighty Forcan Ridge on to the Saddle. The campsite lies in the deep crevice of Glen Shiel, surrounded by these monsters, and it's fair to say that the view from your tent, in all directions, is of steep rock walls heading skywards.

It's a mesmerising place to just sit and stare, without even putting a single foot on the hills. It's a place for dedicated hill-folk, certainly, but hills are only half the story here, because this is a startlingly good area for more generalised exploration.

Besides all those big, brave hills there are plenty of local, lower-level walks, notably the track up Glen Lichd (it goes on and on, with the only limit being your own), or the path over to Glen More on the Glenelg Peninsula, and back via the Mam Ratagan Pass.

Still on an active theme, cyclists have ample opportunities to pedal through terrain varying from the near flat lochside lane on the western side of Loch Duich to a marathon push over to Glenelg and back. Another tremendous on-road biking route takes you around Loch Duich and Loch Long, then up Glen Elchaig to examine the Falls of Glomach which, after heavy rain, are awesome. In truth, the off-road and on-road biking opportunities around Glen Shiel, Glenelg and Loch Duich are almost as endless as the walking routes.

If you're not a hill-walking superhero, what has Shiel Bridge got to offer holidaymakers who aren't so keen on a hamstring hammering? Loads, is the answer. The Glenelg Peninsula is one of the least spoilt and least trodden places in Scotland, and stunningly beautiful, to boot. At Sandaig, you'll find the location where author Gavin Maxwell lived with his otters and wrote the definitive story of solitary life in the Highlands, *Ring of Bright Water*. Then there are the wider attractions of Skye, with a distillery to visit, more waterfalls to gaze at, boat trips galore and, for general touring, the whole of Wester Ross to explore.

That very icon of Scottish scenes, Eilean Donan Castle, lies a few easy pedalling miles along the loch shore, too, but expect to share it with every nationality under the sun, such is this magnificent place's celebrity status on the international tourist circuit.

For a really great day by bike or car, go over the Mam Ratagan Pass, board the tiny car ferry to Skye then meander back through Skye to Kyle of Lochalsh, returning via the (now free) road bridge. A very different kind of journey can be taken on the railway from Kyle of Lochalsh to Inverness, as the train threads its way through one of Europe's most handsome and empty landscapes before arriving in the not-so-big city. If the weather were consistently kinder, all these attractions would make Shiel Bridge the Holy Grail of holidaying places.

The site itself is ever so civilised, with excellent shower and washing facilities, the provision of electric hook-ups and a decent food shop next door. But as at all campsites on the west coast of Scotland, midge protection measures need to be thorough. So, while the atmosphere on the site reeks distinctly of all things mountaineery, it would be unfair to cast the place in such a singular role; Shiel Bridge is just as good as a scenic base-camp as it is as a home for climbing heroes. That said, just see if you can resist the lure of those hills.

THE UPSIDE Totally immersed in magnificent mountainous scenery.
THE DOWNSIDE Totally immersed in cloud and rain quite often.
THE DAMAGE Adults £5; children £2.50. A family of 4 (2 adults, 2 children) costs £12.50 per night. Camper vans and caravans cost £15. Dogs are welcome (free of charge), on the condition that they are well behaved.
THE FACILITIES Modern and comprehensive, with toilets, showers (2 apiece), washbasins and electric hook-ups. There's also a shop and petrol station where you book in, selling most essentials

so you can stock up while you reserve your pitch.
NEAREST DECENT PUB The rather splendidly situated Kintail Lodge Hotel (01599 511275; www.kintaillodgehotel.co.uk) is a half-mile walk from the site, overlooking Loch Duich. It serves decent bar meals and also has a good restaurant serving up a host of local seafood and game.
IF IT RAINS The iconic Eilean Donan Castle (01599 555202; www.eileandonancastle.com) is 6 miles away, or how about a trip on the Seaprobe Atlantis glass bottomed boat (08009 804846; www.seaprobeatlantis.com) from Kyle of Lochalsh?
GETTING THERE Nice and easy. The site is

situated just off the A87(T) Kyle of Lochalsh road behind the shop at Shiel Bridge.
PUBLIC TRANSPORT Scottish Citylink (08705 505050) runs the no. 915 bus from Fort William to Shiel Bridge Junction. The bus journey takes about an hour and a half, but it's then only a 2-minute walk to the site.
OPEN Mar–Oct.
IF IT'S FULL Other good sites in the area include the Caravan Club Site at Morvich (01599 511354) with level pitches surrounded by a stunning mountainscape, or Ardelve Campsite (01599 555231) for views of Eilean Donan Castle.

Shiel Bridge Campsite, Glenshiel, By Kyle of Lochalsh, Ross-shire IV40 8HW

| | t | 01599 511221 | w | www.shielbridgecaravanpark.co.uk | 28 | on the map |

moyle park

The Glenelg Peninsula is a wonderfully detached and independent place hidden from the eyes of the world by a curtain of high, inhospitable mountains. Its shores look out across to Skye and the deep indentation of Loch Hourn that curves around the southern boundary.

Access over the protective mountains is nigh on impossible – even on foot. In just one unlikely-looking place, Mam Ratagan, a narrow road struggles over the hills and drops like a stone into this idyllic spot.

Glenelg is perhaps most famous as the setting for Gavin Maxwell's life (and novel) with his otter, and the place where he lived can be found after a stiff walk to the shore.

Until recently there has been no official campsite in Glenelg, leaving campers who wished to savour the solitude huddled together, wild camping (see p160) on the shore near the ferry across to Skye. The problem with the wild camping was that so many people, from all over Europe, were turning up to experience the peace and quiet of Glenelg that there was none left. It had become more 'beach ghetto' than 'wild'.

Thankfully the small campsite at Moyle Park, a mile or so away from the sea, has recently opened to offer an easier and more peaceful alternative. This simple little site, surrounded by mountains, has basic facilities that blend seamlessly into the stunning surroundings.

THE UPSIDE The site is in the heart of Glenelg – a place of legend to travellers and those who have read or seen *Ring of Bright Water*.
THE DOWNSIDE The difficult journey here, and the lack of ready-made entertainment.
THE DAMAGE £10–12 for tent and occupants. Dogs can come along for free.
THE FACILITIES New (though simple) block with toilets and showers. Freshwater taps and chemical disposal point.
NEAREST DECENT PUB The only pub around is the splendid Glenelg Inn (01599 522273; www.glenelg-inn.com), which is a 4-mile hike from the site. It serves both posh nosh and bar

meals, specialising in locally caught seafood.
IF IT RAINS The ferry across to Skye is run by the residents of Glenelg, and is a thoroughly crazy (but practical) little contraption, so take a trip across the water on it. Otherwise, the only accessible attractions are back out over that steep narrow road. Eilean Donan Castle (01599 555202; www.eileandonancastle.com) is 12 miles away. Further up the valley from the campsite, though not necessarily wet-weather attractions, the Glenelg Brochs (world-famous Iron Age fortified ruins) are nonetheless worth a visit.
GETTING THERE Leave the A87 Kyle of Lochalsh road at Shiel Bridge on to the minor

road to Glenelg over the Mam Ratagan Pass. This is a steep and narrow road requiring a great deal of care. At the bottom of the pass (once you've crossed over the mountains) take the first left, and the campsite is a mile away on the left.
PUBLIC TRANSPORT Buses and trains run to Kyle of Lochalsh, but the nearest bus stop to the campsite is at Shiel Bridge, some 6 hilly miles away.
OPEN All year.
IF IT'S FULL There are no other campsites on the Glenelg Peninsula, but wild camping is tolerated on the shores of Glenelg Bay. The nearest official campsite is Shiel Bridge (p147).

Moyle Park Campsite, Glenelg, Ross-shire IV40 8LA

| t | 01599 522242 | w | www.moyleparkcampsite.co.uk | 29 | on the map |

the wee camp site

As names go, they don't come any more appropriate. The Wee Camp Site does exactly what it says on the tin, offering a stripped-down camping experience on one of the smallest sites in Scotland. The brother and sister owners (who took over from their father after he started the site back in the 1970s) are firmly against the corporate world of onsite shops, bustling bars and infinite rows of caravans. Instead they provide just a sprinkling of grassy shelves where you can pitch up, soak in the views and let the world gently amble by.

The Wee Camp Site hardly ever gets really busy, partly because there aren't enough pitches to apply the term appropriately and partly because few people actually make it here. The exception to this rule is one random week in summer, when a coach-load of Czech campers who have been coming every year for as long as anyone can remember arrives at the site. If you manage to avoid them (perfectly nice as they may be), you may even have the place to yourself.

The unmarked pitches lie on the level terraces that ease down the hillside, allowing you to pitch where you want, though be careful to keep a respectable distance from your fellow campers; cosy Czechs aside, the Wee Camp Site is not keen on packing in tents sardine-style. Through the trees that separate the site from the quiet village of Lochcarron, there are tempting views of the deep, blue expanse of Loch Carron itself. In the other direction, from the rear of the site, the views are of grassy foothills leading off into mountainous terrain. For hikers, the path at the back of the site opens up a massive expanse of unspoiled walks; you can stick to one of the narrow paths or sheep tracks, or simply blaze your own trail. It's a good idea to take all the necessary gear, as there will be nothing else up there but you, the sheep and, invariably, the wind.

Given the lack of facilities, or anything to do on the site itself, the village of Lochcarron tempts. Although not as popular as the tourist star of Plockton, famed as the setting for *Hamish Macbeth* back in the 1990s, on the other side of the loch (itself well worth a visit if you have a car or a bike), Lochcarron is a pleasantly sleepy wee place to while away the hours, with a trim, whitewashed waterfront and a sprinkling of cosy cafés. It even has its own nine-hole golf course, which, though it will never stage the British Open, has sweeping views of the mountains and lochs all around. In every direction are impossibly sturdy and rugged mountains, whether you're looking across at Attadale over the water or off to the west and the mountains of Applecross. The proximity of the campsite to the western coast means that an essential activity around these parts is to tuck into impossibly plump and juicy langoustines, known simply as 'prawns' in these parts. They are so tasty and abundant that many are spirited off to the fine dining tables of London and Paris, though you can savour them locally at the Kishorn Seafood Bar.

The fact that the owners are not embracing mass-market tourism or exploiting peak-season campers with exorbitant rates is obvious as soon as you arrive and pay the more than reasonable bill (£8 per night for a family of four).

So, happily, it's a wee camp site accompanied by suitably wee prices.

THE UPSIDE Does what it says on the tin.
THE DOWNSIDE The unisex facilities are a bit on the basic side.
THE DAMAGE £4 per adult per night. Children are free. Pets are welcome.
THE FACILITIES The basic 2-toilet and 2-shower block with washing machine is a bit dated and basic but does have hot water.
NEAREST DECENT PUB The Lochcarron Hotel (01520 722226), on the main road in Lochcarron, has a decent range of pub grub and a popular beer garden. You won't go wrong if you stick to staples like fish and chips or the daily specials.

IF IT RAINS Visit the nearby Kishorn Seafood Bar (01520 733240), 6 miles to the west in Kishorn, on the way to Applecross, for some of the freshest and best-value seafood you'll taste anywhere in the UK. Well worth the drive or cycle. Alternatively, head to nearby Strathcarron and catch the scenic railway (08457 484950) to either Plockton or Inverness.
GETTING THERE Heading north from Inverness on the A9 take the A835 towards Ullapool then the A832 towards Gairloch and the A890/A896 towards Lochcarron. As you enter the village look out for a sign on the right-hand side directing you

to the Wee Camp Site.
PUBLIC TRANSPORT Catch the train (08457 484950) from Inverness to Strathcarron. Regular buses operate between Strathcarron and Lochcarron.
OPEN Easter–Oct.
IF IT'S FULL Try Applecross Campsite (p157) or further back up the A896 you'll find both Shieldaig Grazing (p199) and Torridon (p201). You can also camp next to the nearby Strathcarron Hotel (01520 722227).

The Wee Camp Site, Croft Road, Lochcarron, Wester Ross IV54 8YA

| t | 01520 722898 | 30 on the map |

applecross

Not many campsites are worth losing your car over. But Applecross is one of them. This glorious escape lies well off the tourist trail, across the infamous Bealach na Ba, which is not so much a road as a rite of passage for Scots, a murderous mountain ordeal that soon sorts out the real cars from the old bangers. And that's exactly what happened on our first visit; our prehistoric Rover never recovered from the experience. But one of the first things we did with the new car was head straight back, because Applecross is that sort of place.

The Bealach na Ba is Scotland's highest road, rising up from sea level to the top of the pass (625 metres high) in a series of hair-raising switchbacks. A large sign cautions that it is not a road for learner drivers and should not be attempted at all in wintry conditions, a message that any Jeremy Clarkson-type will see no doubt as a challenge and put a foot firmly on the accelerator. To make things even more interesting, it is a single-track road with passing places at a premium. You'll not be alone if you find yourself saying your prayers as you 'negotiate' for space with oncoming cars (the locals tend to feel that hurtling up and down with their eyes closed, hoping for the best, is a winning strategy) and the occasional kamikaze bus driver.

For the more cautious driver, there is a road in from the north of the Applecross Peninsula, but it takes a good hour and a half longer and does not have the same heart-stopping 'why-did-we-come-this-way-you-idiot!' drama attached. At the top of the Bealach na Ba, make sure to stop at the parking place, where an orientation board highlights the local landmarks and the multitude of islands and peaks that you can savour all around. That is, of course, if the weather is good; on a bad day you may need a compass just to get back to your car.

The campsite itself is handily located on the road that slaloms down towards the village from the mountain pass. Go past the first field by the reception as the views are better from the 'overflow' field and there are no caravans there. Both fields are relatively flat with soft ground to pitch on, and occupy great positions overlooking Applecross Bay. A deer fence does detract from the view slightly, but some enterprising souls don't let that get in their way and just sling their camping chairs over to the other side. From here you will get some of the finest views you will ever see of Scotland's largest island, Skye, with its world-famous and unmistakable Cuillin Mountains. The site does have a few statics, a B&B and 10 camping huts (eight wishbones and two wigwams) to go along with the space for 60 tents but, aside from the height of summer, it doesn't usually get too crowded, mainly because of the effort required to get here.

Down in the tiny village (little more than a string of whitewashed houses clinging to the seafront) the highlight is the legendary Applecross Inn. This is the hub of the community where locals and visitors mingle over lobster and langoustines (called prawns up here) hauled ashore by the bloke sitting in the corner who now looks a bit worse for wear after a few too many celebratory pints. Yes, you can walk all around the Applecross Peninsula, go out on an adrenaline-filled RIB (rigid inflatable boat) ride and cruise around on a stately sea kayak, but most campers seem to prefer to split their time between the Inn and the campsite (where every year in late summer you can join in an archeological dig) – while their cars sit sweating away in anticipation of the nightmare trip back across the Bealach na Ba.

THE UPSIDE One of Scotland's most remote campsites enjoys a real end-of-the-world feel as well as views of the Isle of Skye.

THE DOWNSIDE The walk back up the hill from the Applecross Inn and the car journey to the site.

THE DAMAGE £6.50 per adult; 12–16-year-olds £3.50; under-12s free. Dogs £1. Nights in the camping huts from £26; dogs £5.

THE FACILITIES Good toilets (8 onsite and a further 3 in the café) with hot showers (6) and a laundry. The funky Flower Tunnel café serves food and drinks (both alcoholic and non alcoholic); it also has a small play area and armchairs.

NEAREST DECENT PUB Pubs just don't get any better than the Applecross Inn (01520 744262). Enjoy fresh-from-the-boat seafood. Lobster, fresh beef and lamb are all regulars on the menu, with real ales on tap and a good selection of wines.

IF IT RAINS Apart from the Applecross Inn, the Potting Shed Café (01520 744440) is worth popping into, if only to see the Victorian walled garden they are trying to resurrect. They serve sandwiches and other hearty snacks during the day, switching to an à la carte menu bursting with local produce and fresh seafood in the evenings.

GETTING THERE From Inverness, continue north on the A9, then the A835 towards Ullapool, followed by the A832 towards Gairloch and the A896 towards Lochcarron. Just past the village of Kishorn, turn left on to the Bealach na Ba, which is clearly signposted.

PUBLIC TRANSPORT It's complicated to say the least. Lochcarron Garage (01520 722205; www.visittorridon.co.uk/travel.htm) runs a service to the Applecross shop from Strathcarron, which in turn can be reached from Inverness by train (08457 484950).

OPEN All year (although don't even think about Bealach na Ba in snowy or icy conditions).

IF IT'S FULL Sheildaig Grazing (p199) isn't too far away, but it's informal camping and doesn't have facilities.

Applecross Campsite, Applecross, Strathcarron, Wester Ross IV54 8ND

| | t | 01520 744268 | w | www.applecross.uk.com/campsite | 31 | on the map |

Wild Camping

Enjoy this epitome of camping
freedom by following a few simple
dos and don'ts.

There's nothing quite like the freedom to roam the land all day and then, when your weary bones finally cry 'enough!', to pitch your tent pretty much wherever you choose – on a lonely hillside, under an old stone bridge or on the dunes of a sandy bay. Through the night there's nothing but you and the stars and in the morning you unzip your tent and look out over a landscape without another soul in sight.

That's the theory of wild camping, anyway...

When Scotland's Land Reform Act was passed in 2003, it was a milestone achievement and a victory for the right of the public to enjoy the land. It was particularly welcomed by campers as it enshrined a right to 'wild camping', defined by the Outdoor Access Code (which came into effect in 2005 to safeguard the newly accessible land) as 'lightweight, done in small numbers and for only two or three nights in any one place'.

Soon after, wild campers hoiked their boots on, packed their tents up and went out and about; staying here, there and everywhere; enjoying the taste of freedom and feeling that everything was right with the world. After all, wild camping's one of the best ways to really get away from it all. You find a charming spot and stay a night or two and, by following the code, leave no trace of ever having been there. It's the perfect form of low-impact tourism.

Except that, unfortunately, it hasn't quite turned out that way.

Because however well behaved we all are when we wild camp, there's a cumulative impact of numbers that eventually begins to take its toll on the popular places where wild campers tend to congregate. Word soon gets around about the best spots and pretty soon more and more tents, camper vans and caravans are arriving to enjoy the place. It's not really anyone's fault, it's just an unavoidable fact, but its impact can be quite destructive.

By the magnificent bay at Horgabost on the Isle of Harris, for example, a few campers started pitching their tents on the dunes. Each year more and more people came to stay, not just for a couple of nights but often for a week or more at a time. Eventually, Scottish Natural Heritage stepped in and asked a local couple to oversee the 'site'.

A portaloo was installed to help with sanitation. The following year, old shipping containers were being converted into male and female facilities and a campers' kitchen set up. Then came a £5 per tent and £10 per caravan fee via an honesty box for staying at this 'wild' site in order to help pay for maintenance. The result? It's still a great place to go but instead of that sense of freedom that wild camping ought to bring, it just feels like any other campsite.

Elsewhere, horror stories abound about black fire scars in the sand dunes, litter being left behind and, most serious of all, accounts of chemical toilets being emptied on to beaches or into the sea.

So, what's the answer? Well, first of all, we all need to stick to the code. Don't stay in one place for more than a few nights, make sure you take all your rubbish away with you and if you do light an open fire, remove the turf beforehand and replace it over the remains in the morning. Remember that wild camping should leave no trace. Second, find your own little patch of paradise. Remember that part of the joy of wild camping is the solitude, so be brave and strike out on your own rather than congregating with loads of other wild campers. You might be surprised at some of the places you find and even more pleased that you can enjoy them all to yourself. And it's for that reason that we've decided not to recommend specific places to wild camp for this edition of **Cool Camping: Scotland**.

Of course, this sort of camping isn't for everyone. You don't have the luxury of toilets or showers for a start – just a shovel and some rain. If you're at all unsure about wild camping you can always try it out at some of the more informal campsites around the country. The free site at Torridon (p201) is a good place to start, or try one of the Western Isles' common grazing sites like Ardroil (p189). Both have only rudimentary facilities and so will give you a taster of life without hot showers and a reception selling fizzy drinks. Then, if you think to yourself that this is the life for you, well then, Scotland's your oyster and away you go.

Nothing quite matches wild camping and hopefully we can keep it that way. By treating the freedom to camp in the wilds of Scotland as a privilege rather than a right, we can keep it enjoyable for everyone. And if you do find that special little place that's wild camping heaven, we won't blame you if you keep it to yourself.

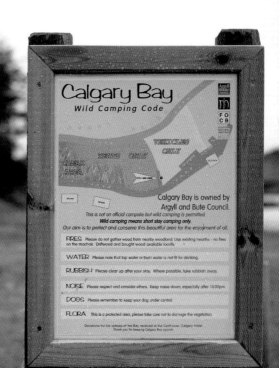

Wild Camping Summary

We could bore you with a load of impenetrable legal guff about the Scottish Outdoor Access Code and the Land Reform (Scotland) Act 2003. Instead, we've chewed it all over and come up with a couple of simple summaries: what it says and what it means.

What It Says

Your Rights: Everyone has the right of access to the land for recreational purposes (including camping), providing that they act responsibly.

Your Responsibilities: (1) Take personal responsibility for your actions and the actions of those under your care (such as children and pets); (2) Respect other people's privacy and peace of mind; and (3) care for the environment.

Where? The Land Reform Act covers most Scottish land, including mountains, moorland, woods and forests, fields and most urban and country parks and open spaces.

The Main Exemptions: You can't camp in: the gardens of private houses; the grounds of castles and historic houses that charge an entry fee; sports centres, pitches and playing fields; schools; the grounds of factories and industrial plants; military bases or land under cultivation. There are other exemptions, such as sewerage works, chemical plants and the like, but you'd be pretty mad to want to camp in them anyway.

What It Means

Wild Camping: The Outdoor Access Code defines wild camping as 'lightweight, done in small numbers and only for two or three nights in any one place.' In other words, it doesn't mean pitching up somewhere with a caravan and awning and spending a fortnight's summer holiday there.

Toilet Training: Where possible, use public lavatories. If you are out in the wilds, follow a couple of simple rules. For a watery stop, ensure you are at least 30 metres from any open water, rivers or streams. For something more substantial, dig a shallow hole as far as possible from any buildings, open water, rivers or streams and farm animals and replace the turf when you're done. And as a matter of etiquette, never ask someone heading for the woods with a shovel what they're up to.

Open Fires: Be aware of any restrictions, due, for example, to a prolonged dry spell (what – in Scotland?) and where possible use a stove instead. Never cut down or damage trees. Keep any open fire small and under control and never leave it unattended. Remove all traces of an open fire before you leave.

Litter: Simple. Don't. Take it all away with you.

Handy Info:
For further information and to download a copy of the code, check out www.outdooraccess-scotland.com. There's also a useful summary of dos and don'ts at the Mountaineering Council of Scotland's website at www.mcofs.org.uk/know-the-code.asp.

sligachan

The western fringe of Scotland is a place completely set apart from the rest of Britain by its remarkable mixture of big, rocky mountains, beautiful lush green valleys and seductive sandy shorelines. Nowhere else soothes the troubled urban soul quite like this northern paradise.

Well, that's the western fringe of Scotland for you, summed up in a sentence or two, but not the Isle of Skye. For this remarkable island is as different from the west of Scotland as the north-western fringe is from the south-east of England. Skye doesn't do soothing, or soft, and Skye certainly doesn't do a lot of green. Skye is elemental, savage, bare, boggy and can be a hard mistress. But like all forms of basic beauty, Skye is completely addictive and once seen (in the right light) eats into your soul and never loses its grip. You spend your southern days waiting for the next trip north, and right in the middle of all this fanciful soul-searching savagery sits Sligachan campsite – a victim and a victory all in one place.

Dealing with sensible, practical matters first, the site's ablutional facilities are acceptable and more than adequate, if not plush. But the squat stone building containing them reflects the harshness of the world outside, and this has somehow crept inside too.

If bad weather persists it also seems to seep inside the mind, but thankfully the weather around here can best be described as 'fast' for no sooner have curtains of mist been drawn across the Cuillins than they're thrust open again by a furious wind bowling in from the bay. But such 'fast' weather is good because it helps hinder the seeming whole world's supply of midges from leaping out of the boggy wastes surrounding the site and brandishing their teeth.

There are good grounds for suggesting that Britain should set up its Olympic Training Village at Sligachan, as several world records are broken on any given evening when the midges are around. It's about 400 metres from the centre of the site to the pub door, and from tent to bar, wearing big boots and anorak, it takes the average camper 19.8 seconds to cover the distance with a million midges in hot pursuit. Astounding.

If you're getting the impression that we're attempting to put you off a visit to Sligachan then there may be some truth in that assumption, but we do believe in painting a true picture of things. It is, of course, almost incidental that we might want the place to ourselves, for when things turn out right here, when the sun shines (and those pesky midge adversaries can't stand the heat, muwahahaha!), then we who have been victims want to enjoy the spoils exclusively. And when things are right, some of the roughest, rockiest, most savage scenes on the island sit directly behind the hotel and campsite, daring you to dip even a toe into their territory. And dip it you must as the walking around here offers abundant visual rewards, especially from the Cuillins.

Even getting to Sligachan from the Skye Bridge is an experience always remembered, as the road winds through the big hills of the Red Cuillins into the very centre of the island, where the campsite and the fearful-looking Black Cuillins await your flimsy nylon. But the most outrageous thing about Skye is that the most outrageous scenes of all, up on the Trotternish Peninsula and all around the pinnacled northern coast, haven't even been glimpsed as yet.

No, Skye isn't comfortable, but it's a place worth persevering the pain to discover, and Sligachan is the place to gainfully employ yourselves in that process.

THE UPSIDE Slap bang in the centre of the craziest scenery in the realm.
THE DOWNSIDE Slap bang in the centre of the craziest midge-breeding scenery in the realm.
THE DAMAGE £5 per adult, children 5–13 years £3 and under-5s free. Dogs permitted too.
THE FACILITIES A bit rough and ready for some, but the site is reasonably equipped with showers, toilets, washbasins, electric hook-ups, washing machine and tumble-dryer.
NEAREST DECENT PUB One of the great pubs

of the world, the Sligachan Hotel (01478 650204), with its quiet and cosy MacKenzies Bar inside or livelier Seumas Bar adjacent, is directly across the road. They serve enormous meals, a baffling variety of ales (mostly brewed onsite at the hotel's own micro-brewery) and every variety of Scotch known to (Scots) man. The atmosphere in the Seumas Bar is terrific too.
IF IT RAINS See 'Nearest Decent Pub'. The hotel also has a small 'museum' of collected documents charting the hotel's history from 1913.

GETTING THERE The site is next to the main road running up through Skye (A850) from the bridge to Portree.
PUBLIC TRANSPORT Bus no. 50C goes directly from Portree Square to the Sligachan Hotel. Contact Traveline (08712 002233; www.travelinescotland.com) for times.
OPEN Easter–Oct.
IF IT'S FULL Glenbrittle (p173) lies across the other side of this colossal pile of island scenery.

Sligachan Campsite, Sligachan, Isle of Skye IV47 8SW

| | | t | 07786 435294 or the hotel: 01478 650204 | w | www.sligachan.co.uk | 32 | on the map |

glenbrittle

When was the last time you saw the Milky Way? Or had no signal on your mobile? In this remote glen on the Isle of Skye, far away from the ubiquitous glow of sodium street lamps and the tinny clamour of downloaded ringtones, a hazy white ribbon stretches across the clear and silent night sky. If you watch for long enough you're bound to see the streak of a shooting star and if you listen carefully enough you'll hear nothing at all. It's an ideal opportunity to reacquaint yourself with constellations you know only from newspaper horoscopes, and with the pleasures of total silence.

Glenbrittle is not one of those sites with shiny toilet blocks, tumble-dryers and chiller cabinets full of fizzy drinks for the kids. This vast tract of Skye, complete with its own lengthy paddle-friendly beach, is owned by the MacLeod clan who gained public prominence a few years ago by trying to sell the Cuillin Mountains for the bargain price of £10 million. Curiously, buyers were thin on the ground. The facilities at Glenbrittle have been upgraded, and the number of pitches has risen by 20, but the rugged simplicity of the site still abounds to attract those in need of some serious R&R. It is a little like a links golf course, with smooth broad fairways in which to pitch your tent and knee-deep rough in which to lose stray tent pegs.

If you do misplace any, the gregarious Alex MacGregor, who runs the campsite's shop, will sell you some replacements. Alex is one of those annoyingly sunny people who are the envy of city dwellers. He spends half the year amid the beauty of Glenbrittle and the other half travelling in Asia. His worldly ways are useful in a site that attracts an eclectic clientele from all corners of the world. You may stumble upon Scottish hippies singing 'Ziggy Stardust' around a fire on the beach, cooking up the mussels they've collected from the shore; a gaggle of Polish climbers returning to the site from the Cuillin Hills, jangling their crampons and carabiners; or a quiet Japanese couple with a state-of-the-art tent and a worrying collection of sashimi knifes. Just don't let them see the Pot Noodle you're cooking up for your own supper.

Those of a healthy disposition should visit the Fairy Pools, a few miles back up the single-track road that leads to Glenbrittle. This series of mountain pools and streams sits in the lee of the mountains and, though the water is freezing even in summer, a breathless dip here has more restorative power than the swankiest health spa, and you can always arm yourself with a wetsuit to keep the goosebump count down. If you have been climbing the mountains above, the pools provide the perfect opportunity to cool down before heading back to camp.

Glenbrittle is probably most popular with climbers, who use it as a base for tackling the Cuillins, the mountain range that dominates the Skye skyline. Like a jaw full of broken and blackened teeth, it looms over Glenbrittle, blotting out the early sun. Every morning, plucky climbers can be seen setting off up the hill at dawn but quickly look as small as hobbits against the mountains. Climbing here is a serious business and not for the fainthearted. But even if you are not part of the crampon and carabiner crew, Glenbrittle is the perfect tonic for anyone who wants peace, tranquillity and a mobile phone with no signal.

THE UPSIDE Great views of the Milky Way and free mussels on the beach.
THE DOWNSIDE It's tricky to get to outside of the summer months if you're a car-less camper, with buses few and far between.
THE DAMAGE £5.50 per adult and £3.50 per child (5–15 years); under-5s go free. There are now 9 electric hook-ups at £4 each.
THE FACILITIES The rustic wash block has undergone a refurb and boasts an upgraded boiler for good hot showers. Drinking water is available and there's an outdoor dishwashing area with a single cold tap.

The campsite shop is well stocked with provisions and even climbing equipment.
NEAREST DECENT PUB The Old Inn (01478 640205) at Carbost, 8 miles back up the single-track access road, has regular live music throughout the summer and a lively atmosphere. For those who prefer fine ales or single malts, try either of the bars at the Sligachan Hotel (01478 650204).
IF IT RAINS Visit the Talisker Distillery (01478 614308) at Carbost. Talisker is one of the smokiest, peatiest malts around.
GETTING THERE From the Skye Bridge follow the A87 to Sligachan. Turn left on to the A863 at the sign for Dunvegan. After 5 miles, turn left for Carbost on the B8009 and follow the road for 2 miles until the sign for Glenbrittle and take the single-track road down to the sea.
PUBLIC TRANSPORT Bus no. 53 runs from Portree to Glenbrittle. It's run by Highland Country (01463 222244) and goes twice a day in summer.
OPEN Apr–Sep.
IF IT'S FULL There is a youth hostel (08700 041121) a few miles back up the road and the Waterside Bunkhouse at the Old Inn (01478 640205) at Carbost.

Glenbrittle Campsite, Carbost, Isle of Skye IV47 8TA

| t | 01478 640404 | w | www.dunvegancastle.com | 33 | on the map |

kinloch

Kinloch's a popular place name in Scotland. It means 'head of the loch', but you need to make sure you end up at the right head of the right loch. Sometimes it's easy enough, if you're heading for Kinlochbervie or Kinlochleven, for example. But there are at least five straightforward Kinlochs in Scotland and the one you're looking for here is in northern Skye, right on the shores of Loch Dunvegan.

The beauty of Kinloch campsite is that it attracts all sorts, from Dutch-registered Land Rovers and passing Harleys and Triumphs to classic wooden caravans from the days when caravanning was an upper-class pursuit and its adherents were known as 'gentleman vagabonds'. The motors and two-wheelers are mainly confined to the front of the site (where there are some hard standings), while tents have the run of the grassy banks round the side.

The site is owned and run by Colin and Peggy Campbell, and ably assisted by the avuncular Archie. Colin's a man of Skye, born and bred, with a wry but engaging outlook on life, who seems happy to while away the time chatting about this and that.

You can't quite get down to the loch's shore because there's a fence to keep the sheep at bay, but you're close enough to hear the lapping water and have a seal's eye view across to the whitewashed village and its prominent church, while on the hilltop above is a single standing stone, a guard perhaps, keeping watch over the 'head of the loch'.

THE UPSIDE Pretty lochside location in remote northern Skye.
THE DOWNSIDE Can get fairly windy and the site's quite undulating.
THE DAMAGE £6 per per adult per night, kids under 12 are £1. Electricity is £4. Dogs are free, but please keep them on a lead.
THE FACILITIES One very clean and respectable block with 3 hot showers and 3 WCs each for campers male and female. There's plenty of dishwashing capacity with hot water and a washing machine (£2.50) and dryer (£1), as well as an iron. The site will also recharge phones, camera batteries, iPods and other bits for free.

NEAREST DECENT PUB There are 2 bars in Dunvegan, both attached to hotels – the Misty Isle (01470 521208) and the rather dull Dunvegan Hotel (01470 521497). Head instead the 7 miles to Waternish and the Stein Inn (01470 592362). Skye's oldest pub is in a beautiful row of whitewashed houses right next to the lochside.
IF IT RAINS Dunvegan Castle (01470 521206; www.dunvegancastle.com) is the ancient seat of the Clan MacLeod, which still owns large tracts of Skye. It's the oldest continuously inhabited castle in Scotland (the current MacLeod of MacLeod is the 30th in the line) so as you'd expect there's a wealth of history on display. It's open Apr–Oct

and costs £7.50 per adult; £4 for kids.
GETTING THERE Follow the A87 from north or south to Carbost and take the A850 for Dunvegan. Enter the village down the hill, turn sharp left at the Dunvegan Hotel, past the post office and turn right at the sign for Glendale (the B884). The site entrance is on a steep left-hand bend just beyond the bridge.
PUBLIC TRANSPORT There are 3 buses a day from Portree to Dunvegan and then it's a ½ mile walk.
OPEN Apr–end Oct.
IF IT'S FULL Head north to Camus More (p179) or south back to Sligachan (p169).

Kinloch Campsite, Dunvegan, Isle of Skye IV55 8WQ

| t | 01470 521531 | w | www.kinloch-campsite.co.uk | 34 on the map |

camus more

The Isle of Skye has always been one of the more romantic spots of Scotland, the epitome of the tartan and heather view of the Highlands and Islands. This is partly because it's always been the most accessible island from the mainland, so it's a little more well known – and well worn – than the outer isles. Even before the stylish Skye Bridge was built and the tolls abolished, Skye was only a short ferry trip from Kyle of Lochalsh. And it was the first of the Hebrides to have Sunday sailings, in 1964; something that still causes controversy with other islands today.

Skye's reputation is for its scenery, from the ragged Cuillins to the ridges of Trotternish, and for its association with Bonnie Prince Charlie. After his defeat at the Battle of Culloden in 1746, the fleeing prince, dressed in drag, was rowed across from Benbecula by a local lass, Flora MacDonald. He gave her a locket in thanks and hoped they'd meet again. They never did. He fled to live out his days as an exile in Rome while she was arrested and sent to the Tower of London. Though she was later released and emigrated to North Carolina, she's gone down in history as a plucky and rosy-cheeked heroine.

Camus More, in the small crafting community of Bornesketaig, has been in the MacDonald family for four generations and Iain and Bryony have lived here full time since 1989. They started up the small campsite a good 20-odd years ago, but have managed to keep it fairly under the radar (they don't own a computer so have no website), known only to a small band of aficionados and the occasional lost soul who stumbles here by mistake.

There are only a dozen or so pitches, shaved out of the long grass and separated from the beach by a low stone wall. The site is on the Ray Mears side of basic with just a couple of loos and an outdoor sink for washing – and it's cold water only – but then somehow it seems in keeping with the sparse surroundings. Behind the site the land sweeps slowly upwards, dotted with houses from the old to the new, up towards the cliffs of the Trotternish Ridge. This jagged range defines the north of Skye as surely as the Cuillins do the south. There's a grand road right up through the middle of the mountains that's worth trying (by bike if you're feeling fit and brave) for the fantastic views down the eastern side of Skye and out over Staffin Island.

From the site at Camus More, if you're lucky or patient, probably both, you might spot a golden eagle over the hills to the south, a family of otters round the headland or even the occasional school of basking sharks out in the bay, though more likely you'll just get stared at by all the cows in the back field.

If you're not treated to a show by the local wildlife, then you can at least expect a great sunset, so have your camera at the ready. The site looks straight across the Little Minch towards Harris and the Uists, and as the long summer evenings draw to a close here, the sun sinks down behind the line of the Outer Hebrides and you can almost count the islands poking from the fiery sea as they taper off to the south. It's classic Skye, and this is why people who've been can't help but be drawn back again.

After more excitement in North Carolina during the American War of Independence, Flora MacDonald came home and ended her days here, perhaps enjoying the very same sunset views. She's buried on the hill behind the site, a romantic end to a romantic life on the oh-so-romantic Isle of Skye.

THE UPSIDE A true taste of the remote crofting life in one of the lesser-known parts of Skye.
THE DOWNSIDE The lack of hot water or showers makes it a bit hard-core.
THE DAMAGE A tent with 2 adults costs £6. The price goes up depending on extra campers.
THE FACILITIES They're fairly basic. There's 1 male and 1 female WC with washbasin and cold water only. There's an outside twin sink with a drinking-water tap and a shed with table and chairs, a fridge and a couple of power points for battery/mobile recharging. No electric hook-ups.
NEAREST DECENT PUB The Duntulm Castle

Hotel (01470 552213; www.duntulmcastle.co.uk), which is fine for a pint but isn't that great. A better option is to BYOB and make your own fun.
IF IT RAINS The Flora MacDonald memorial and the Skye Museum of Island Life (01470 552206; www.skyemuseum.co.uk) is over the hill and worth a visit for anyone who's ever heard of Bonnie Prince Charlie being rowed in a boat over the sea to Skye.
GETTING THERE From Uig at the end of the A87 follow the A855 towards Kilmuir. At Kilvaxter turn left at the signpost for Bornesketaig. Follow the road down the hill and turn left at the wee

crossroads (by the red postbox). The site's by the sea on the right.
PUBLIC TRANSPORT The no. 57 (A or C) bus does a loop past Kilmuir from Portree. Details of timetables are available at www.stagecoach.com. From Kilmuir it's a mile's walk to the site.
OPEN Mid May–mid Sept.
IF IT'S FULL There's a site behind the ferry terminal at Uig called Uig Bay (01470 542714), which is fine for a night or 2. Otherwise head back to Kinloch (p177).

Camus More, Kilmuir, Isle of Skye IV51 9YS

| | t | 01470 552312 | 35 on the map |

lickisto blackhouse

Harvey and John, owners of Lickisto Blackhouse, invite me to Sunday dinner. Harvey cooks a luscious pork loin stuffed with lemon and ginger with roast potatoes and veggie trimmings. We share a bottle of Co-op claret. Then after a dessert of local pan-fried strawberries with melted soya chocolate, John gets his power tools out.

'Feel the gearing on that', he says. He reaches across the dinner table and hands me a cordless drill. I give the trigger a squeeze and sure enough it's a powerful beast. 'Japanese', he says, and hands me another, German this time. I'm not quite sure what to say. 'Smoother action, definitely', I venture. 'Aye, but not the same power', says John, as if that settles it. I weigh them both in my hands, firing up each in turn before thinking it safer to hand them back and finish my plate of strawberries.

Harvey and John are a bit like that. Harvey's a fancy cook and bakes fresh bread for the camping guests every day before going off to work at his hair salon in Tarbert while John does all the handywork. Since acquiring Lickisto Blackhouse a few years ago, they've been slowly converting the place – the croft they live in, the old blackhouse and a couple of byres – into one of the finest little campsites in the country.

In the desert moonscape of eastern Harris, where the soil's a millimetre thick and the gneiss rock is so hard even a Japanese power drill wouldn't make much of a scratch, they've created what seems like an oasis amid the lifeless land. There are willows and pines, reeds swaying in the wind, a vegetable plot (help yourself) and various grassy pitches secreted away on the croft's 13 acres. Down by the sea loch there's a small landing cove if you want to turn up by boat or if you fancy having a waterside campfire of an evening.

More likely you'll want to spend some of the time in the former weaver's blackhouse, which now forms a snug for the campers. With a couple of sofas arranged by the iron fire (burning peat John cuts himself) and a long communal breakfast table, adorned each morning with the freshly baked bread and eggs (when the hens can be bothered), it's the social hub of the place where you can take a pew and, if you fancy the company, have a chat. Be warned, though, that things can go on well into the early hours if there are a few bottles of wine being passed about.

Around the communal table you're as likely to be rubbing shoulders with cyclists, canoeists and walkers as with people who've come by car. And with room for only one

camper van and no caravans or motorhomes, you're not going to be bothered by the sound of engines in the morning. The whole ethos of the place is as low impact and environmentally friendly as possible.

Lickisto is on the eastern coast by what's known as the Golden Road. That's not because it's spectacular but because it cost an absolute fortune to build across such tricky terrain. On the other side of the island it's a totally different experience: with the prevailing weather battering wind and water against the coast, the western side of Harris is a land of huge sweeping bays with golden sands and water that's travel-brochure blue. Head over to Seilebost for a breathtaking example that, on a good day, will have you swearing you're somewhere in the Caribbean. Or just stay at Lickisto to chill out amid the greenery and quiet, broken only by the sound of the occasional power drill.

THE UPSIDE A stunning oasis in the lunar landscape of Harris.
THE DOWNSIDE It's a touch pricier than the local average. But then it's not an average site.
THE DAMAGE It's £10 per person per night and £5 for kids up to a certain height (defined arbitrarily by John). Dogs are welcome and are free of charge.
THE FACILITIES Mind your head, they're through a low entrance into one of the byres. A couple of WCs (including one medieval-looking thing in the corner of its own byre) and 2 decent and sizeable showers. In the blackhouse you'll find a 2-hob gas stove, kettle, toaster and washing-up facilities plus a couple of sofas and a long breakfast table.

NEAREST DECENT PUB Back in Tarbert there's the bar at the Hotel Hebrides (01859 502364; www.hotelhebrides.com). It used to be a dive but has been done up to look like a Battersea wine bar.
IF IT RAINS Well there's always the peat fire in the blackhouse, but if you want to go offsite, no trip to the Outer Hebrides would be complete without a visit to the Standing Stones at Calanais (Callanish). Although this ring of ancient stones (older than Stonehenge) is out of doors, there's an impressive visitor centre (01851 621422; www.callanishvisitorcentre.co.uk) with an exhibition and café. The downside is that it's 40 miles or so north of Lickisto on the Isle of Lewis, so it's a day trip, but a worthwhile one.

GETTING THERE From Tarbert take the A859 south, heading for Leverburgh. After about 4½ miles turn left at the sign for Roghadal. Follow the single-track road for 2½ miles, cross the bridge and, as you climb the hill, just before the bus stop, turn left. There are small discreet camping signs to help direct you.
PUBLIC TRANSPORT The W13 bus runs from Tarbert Pier to Leverburgh, stopping not far from the campsite if you ask for Lickisto.
OPEN Usually around springtime but by arrangement you can stay any time of the year.
IF IT'S FULL Booking is advisable but there is a semi-wild site with an honesty box at Horgabost (see Wild Camping, p160) on the west coast of Harris, right on the dunes.

Lickisto Blackhouse, 1 Lickisto, Isle of Harris HS3 3EL

| | t | 01859 530485 | w | www.freewebs.com/vanvon | 36 | on the map |

ardroil grazing

Look into my eyes, not around my eyes, look into my eyes, and three-two-one you're falling fast asleep...

When you wake up you will forget that you have heard of a beautiful, unspoiled, remote campsite on a simple piece of flat machair beside a mile of tidal sands. You will forget that it has no facilities beyond a couple of public WCs and a water tap and that it is, quite simply, lovely. You won't remember that, when the tide comes in, there's an expanse of knee-deep water that's ideal for an idle paddle, or that when the tide goes out there's a swathe of sand that stretches nearly a mile out to the waves. Neither will it occur to you that you've seen a couple of whitewashed crofts and some grazing cows across the bay, nor that behind you are the mountains. You won't realise that there's absolutely nothing here to spoil the view.

When you wake up, you will forget that you've ever heard of the beauties of the Ardroil Grazings Committee campsite and you will never, ever, go there. Because if you go, you'll enjoy it and then tell other people about it, and then it won't be just our little secret anymore. So, when you wake up, you'll forget everything you've just read.

Three-two-one and you're back in the room. So, you were saying you're off to Skegness for your holidays this year? How lovely.

THE UPSIDE It's an unspoiled piece of grazing land beside a spectacular bay.
THE DOWNSIDE It won't always be unspoiled. Plus the lack of facilities means it's not going to be for everyone.
THE DAMAGE £2 per person per night (this may go up to £3). Dogs are welcome – so long as they're not of the sheep-chasing variety – and won't cost a penny to stay.
THE FACILITIES Minimal: there are a couple of public toilets 100 metres from the sands with a cold water pipe, but that's it.
NEAREST DECENT PUB You need to BYOB. If you've come without, stock up at the Uig Community Shop, which has a decent range of tempting tipples.
IF IT RAINS In keeping with its semi-wild camping status and remote location, there isn't really much in the vicinity apart from the great outdoors, so this is tricky. Play cards, perhaps? Tell funny stories about Auntie Ida?
GETTING THERE Take the A858 from Stornoway and turn left on to the B8011 heading for Miabhig. Carry on through Timsgarry (Timsgearraidh) and you'll see signs for the beach as you climb the hill at Ardroil. Turn left at the sign up to the house to pay, then take the track to the right to the site.
PUBLIC TRANSPORT Bus no. W4 runs from Stornoway to Ardroil, usually twice a day. Call Maclennan Coaches (01851 702114) for details.
OPEN All year.
IF IT'S FULL There's always Cnip Grazing (p191) a few miles back up the road.

Ardroil Grazings Committee, c/o D Mathieson, 6 Ardroil, Timsgarry, Isle of Lewis HS2 9EU

| | | t | 01851 672248 | 37 | on the map |

cnip grazing

If you've never felt like you've reached the end of the earth then come to Traigh na Beirigh (don't try to pronounce it) near Cnip (pronounced 'neep'). This tiny crofting community on the western coast of Lewis in the Outer Hebrides seems like the last place on earth. In reality, if you'd kept on going west you'd eventually end up on the Labrador Coast of Newfoundland (where there's probably someone looking east feeling the same as you) but you'd never guess it standing on the dunes of Traigh na Beirigh gazing out over the aqua-blue water. It feels like the end of everywhere you've ever been. And that, of course, is the attraction. Even the cluster of cottages that comprise Cnip is over the hill in the neighbouring bay, so the only thing to disturb the peace is that occasional bang of a grousing gun in the hills behind and the sound of the waves on the beach.

Traigh na Beirigh is the name of the bay on whose grassy dunes the campsite sits. The site is owned by the Cnip villagers through a community trust and is administered by Agnes Maclennan, a charming woman who lives at number 15. Visitors are ushered into her home while she writes out a receipt for the camping fees. She keeps a warm kitchen, even in the summer, where the heat

of the old Aga and Agnes' lilting west-coast accent, a mix of Scots and Irish, could lull even an insomniac to sleep.

Cnip is 40 miles from Lewis's only real town, Stornoway, over miles and miles of captivating emptiness in which rocks poke up through the threadbare soil like elbows through an old tweed jacket. Agnes's burning Aga is a sign that, even in the summer, the weather on Lewis can be cold and harsh, and the landscape elemental and bleak. And so the bay, when it comes, is something of a surprise. The road from Cnip climbs the shoulder of the hill and as you crest the brow the brilliant blue of the bay is suddenly there before you with its scimitar of white sand fringed with grass.

Compared with some of Scotland's other bays, though, Traigh na Beirigh is modest. If you really want to stretch your legs, then head for Uig Sands, four miles south of Cnip. It's an extravagant cove where the low tide retreats for miles out to sea and leaves a rippled tract of golden sand. It was here that a cow accidentally found the Lewis Chessmen in 1831. Made by the Vikings from walrus ivory, these 12th-century chess pieces were discovered among the sands and are now in the National Museum in Edinburgh.

Old though the ancient chessmen are, even they are new kids on the block in comparison with Lewis' main attraction, the Standing Stones at Calanais (Callanish). These swirling spires of Lewisian gneiss, the oldest rock in Britain, have the gnarled look of petrified oak trunks. As well they might because the stones, set in the shape of a Celtic cross, are older than Stonehenge and just as baffling. The runic allure of them attracts its fair share of hiking hippies, the rocky equivalent of tree-huggers, who come to commune with the stones, much to the frustration of photographers in search of that cherished shot (and much to the amusement of the incurious sheep). Neither can ruin the simple grandeur of Calanais, though, particularly as dusk begins to fall. If you can get a shot of the stones at sunset, it will definitely be one to keep.

And back at Cnip, sunrise over the waters of the bay is another finger-clicking moment to cherish long after you've gone home to tell your friends all about your stay at the end of the earth.

THE UPSIDE Stunning setting at the very end of the world.

THE DOWNSIDE The empty caravans of the Stornoway Caravan Club are parked at the site over the summer, and it can get rather crowded during the peak months.

THE DAMAGE Small (2-person) tent £6; larger tents and camper vans start from £7 per night. Well-behaved dogs are welcome.

THE FACILITIES One recently renovated, small but serviceable, toilet block with male and female facilities (1 cubicle and 2 new £1-coin-operated showers each) and a dishwashing station. There is a recycling facility behind the toilet block.

NEAREST DECENT PUB There are more churches than there are pubs on Lewis. The Uig Community Shop 4 miles south of Cnip at Timsgarry is licensed and sells a decent range of beers, wines and spirits.

IF IT RAINS Think up new similes for the sound of rain on your tent. Like popcorn popping in a pan, for example. Or wander around the stones at Calanais in the rain for an even earthier experience.

GETTING THERE From Stornoway follow the A859 to Leurbost and turn right to Achmor. Then take the B1011 to Miabhig. Take a right and follow the road through Cliobh to Cnip. Stop at house number 15 at the bottom of the hill to pay.

PUBLIC TRANSPORT There is a bus service (no. W4) from Stornoway to Uig with a separate service for the loop road through Cnip.

OPEN Apr–Oct.

IF IT'S FULL Ardroil Grazing (p189) is an informal camping area about 5 miles south at Uig Sands.

Cnip Village Grazing Trust Campsite, Cnip, Uig, Isle of Lewis HS2 9HS		
	t 01851 672265	38 on the map

sands holiday centre

Sands Holiday Centre may have a whopping 150 tent pitches, 160 pitches for touring caravans and (come closer so no one else can hear) is even home to 18 static caravans. But as you pitch among the machair, amid voluminous sand dunes, and linger at the epic view over the Atlantic to the Isle of Skye and the Outer Hebrides you will soon realise that despite its best efforts, the Sands cannot help being a cool place to camp.

This spacious site, flanked by farmland on two sides and the Atlantic on another, allows campers plenty of space even when it gets busy, as owners William and Moira Cameron insist that tents are kept at least seven metres apart. There are no fixed pitches at Sands so you can even set up your tent among the enormous dunes that separate the beach and the campsite. Caravans are banned from this part of the site, so those with tents really do get the prime location and the most appealing views. As you turn your back on the caravans and take in the panorama of the Atlantic and the Outer Hebrides you will soon forget that your fellow campers even exist.

Facilities at the Sands Holiday Centre are plentiful if a little outdated. One of the toilet blocks has been modernised and has underfloor heating, which comes in handy during those cooler nights at the start of the season. A herd of Highland cattle and the Camerons' sheep are added attractions for children, but the real reason to camp here is Little Sands Beach.

Located next to miles of sandy beach that is sheltered by the mass of Longa Island, it is no surprise that the Sands Holiday Centre is popular with water-sports enthusiasts, who arrive with windsurfboards, sailing dinghies and kayaks in tow. The water temperature, somewhat cruelly, rarely rises above 12°C, so don't forget to pack a wetsuit or, even better, a dry suit if you want to spend more than just a few minutes splashing around in the sea. Strong Atlantic breezes can also whip up the waves and the beach does not have a lifeguard, so young children need to be supervised. For landlubbers, Little Sands is a quiet venue for a bracing stroll, for walking the dog or simply watching the world go by. Down on the beach, away from the delicate ecosystem of the dunes, you are even welcome to light a campfire.

If you can bear to drag yourself away from Little Sands Beach make a beeline for the Inverewe Gardens, which are just nine miles away. When Osgood MacKenzie declared his intention to create a garden brimming with exotic plants from around the globe many of his contemporaries thought he'd taken leave of his senses (a belief that his daily skinny dip did nothing to dispel), particularly in light of the fact that his proposed site on the shore of Loch Ewe was comprised mainly of bedrock. His detractors, however, simply did not have the vision to realise that the warm currents that passed through the loch from the Gulf Stream were ideal for what MacKenzie had in mind. Today the verdant gardens at Inverewe boast everything from Californian dog's-tooth violets to Chinese rhododendrons and are widely regarded as some of the most impressive in Britain.

Heading back to Sands Holiday Centre, the first thing you will see are caravans spread around the site, but this time you'll know that up by the dunes lies a camping oasis and you'll soon be hunkering down on the beach enjoying a campfire with epic Highland and Island views.

THE UPSIDE Tent-only camping in the sand dunes with terrific views.
THE DOWNSIDE The 160 touring caravan pitches and 18 static caravans near the entrance.
THE DAMAGE Tent and car plus 2 adults is £12 low season, £14 high season (Jul and Aug). Extra adults are £5 per night and kids (5–15 years old) are £2. Dogs are welcome as long as they're kept on a lead.
THE FACILITIES Hot showers, dishwashing area, electric hook-ups, laundry, payphones, games room, play area and licensed shop.
NEAREST DECENT PUB The Melvaig Inn

(01445 771212), 6 miles from the campsite at Melvaig, is a bar/restaurant with leather sofas, pool table and wonderful views out to Skye. It serves up sandwiches and Ploughman's lunches, as well as cream teas and cakes during the day, then in the evening you can choose from home-made pies and locally caught seafood dinners.
IF IT RAINS The Gairloch Heritage Museum (01445 712287) is open from April to the end of October and welcomes casual visitors seeking shelter, as well as more serious scholars of history. The hands-on exhibits give a good insight into Highland life.

GETTING THERE Take the A832 to Gairloch. From there follow the B8021 coastal road north towards Melvaig. The Sands Holiday Centre is 4 miles along this road on the left.
PUBLIC TRANSPORT There is a daily bus from Inverness to Gairloch. From there you will need to walk or hitch a ride to cover the 4 miles to the site.
OPEN Apr–Oct.
IF IT'S FULL Try the Gairloch Caravan Park (01445 712373) in Strath, 2 miles back down the road towards Gairloch.

Sands Holiday Centre, Gairloch, Wester Ross IV21 2DL

| t | 01445 712152 | w | www.sandscaravanandcamping.co.uk | 39 on the map |

shieldaig grazing

Come and have a graze at Shieldaig. You'll be vying with the sheep for the choicest grass, but this intimate little strip of village grazing land is quite a treat. Sitting on the hill just above the one-street village of Shieldaig, the site overlooks a bay with a wooded *Swallows and Amazons*-style island plonked invitingly in the middle and a couple of wee boats anchored in the still waters. Behind you loom the dark peaks of the Torridon Range, which make for challenging climbing or just a brooding presence at your back as you cook dinner over the campfire.

Shieldaig's on the shores of its own loch, an inlet of Loch Torridon that eats into the land of Wester Ross. Come through the dramatic valley from Kinlochewe in the east and you'll pass under Beinn Eighe, a black monster of a mountain that has seen better days and is now a great stack of crumbling rock that looks about ready to fall apart.

If you reach Shieldaig in one piece you'll find a row of neat whitewashed houses just a stone's throw from the coastal road and right on the lochside. The campsite's pretty small and there's no way to book, so it's advisable to get there early and stake a claim, particularly when the annual fête and music festival is on in late July. After all, you wouldn't want to run the gauntlet through the black valley and have nowhere to graze, or gaze from, at the end of the day.

THE UPSIDE Small informal site with great views over an island in the bay.
THE DOWNSIDE It does attract free-loaders and can get a bit soggy after rain.
THE DAMAGE There's an honesty box for donations. Dogs are allowed on the site.
THE FACILITIES None at the site, though there's a well-maintained public loo with hot and cold water down the hill by the village as well as a drinking-water tap.
NEAREST DECENT PUB The Shieldaig Bar and Coastal Kitchen (01520 755251) is the best option. Down the hill and along the road, it's on the left. Recently rebuilt, it's still fairly small and intimate and tends to be busy (especially when it's raining).
IF IT RAINS Hate to say it, but go to the pub.
GETTING THERE From the A835 between Inverness and Ullapool, take the A832 through Achnasheen to Kinlochewe and the A896 past Torridon. Turn off at Shieldaig and you'll find the site on top of the hill.

PUBLIC TRANSPORT There are bus services to Sheildaig run by DMK (01520 722682) and Lochcarron Garage (01520 722205; book the night before to ensure a seat). Best check www. visittorridon.co.uk/travel.htm for details of times. Out of season, some services are by request only.
OPEN All year.
IF IT'S FULL The free site at Torridon (p201) is back up the road and the Wee Camp Site (p153) is further down the road. And in between is Applecross (p157).

Shieldaig Grazing Committee, Shieldaig, Wester Ross IV54 8XN | 40 on the map

torridon

If the thought of spending the night without a hot shower or flushing toilet makes your blood curdle, but you fancy the freedom of wild camping (see p160), then you're in a bit of a quandary. The solution is on hand, though, in the form of the Torridon campsite. Open only to tents and often deserted, this gem is as close to wild camping as you can get, but with toilets and hot showers on hand to ease you through the experience.

Despite being located just off the A896 at the entrance to Torridon village and opposite the Torridon Countryside Centre, this small field still manages to feel both incredibly remote and rustic. Rowan trees and Scots pines shield the campsite from the road, and the basic toilet and shower block is actually located just outside the main gate – although they belong to the campsite they are also open to the public. The fact that you are allowed to build campfires – as long as you contain them, use twigs and branches that are lying on the ground and don't cut any wood from the trees – is also a big plus. The campsite's crowning glory, though, is the voluminous Liathach massif that looms large from above the northern perimeter; although Torridon's volatile weather and frequent low cloud cover mean that you might only see the boulder fields on the mountain's lower slopes.

In keeping with wild camping, you cannot book a pitch in advance and there is no charge to stay at Torridon. In fact, the only drawback you might face is that it can get boggy if it's been raining, so pitch on the perimeter and park in the Countryside Centre car park. Also, in overcast weather with little wind, the midges can be ferocious, so bring your Avon Skin So Soft repellent (see p211).

Torridon, a mesmerising, protected landscape of sweeping sea lochs, tumbling burns and hulking mountain peaks that vault towards the heavens, is one of Scotland's last great wildernesses and a Mecca for walkers and climbers. Together, the Achnashellach and Torridon hills boast no less than 17 Munros (see Walks and Wheel Trails, p91). The views from the top of Torridon's peaks are breathtaking; however, these are serious mountains, where wild weather, knife-edge ridges and vertical ascents make them hazardous for even the most experienced climber, so caution needs to be exercised.

It is advisable to tackle more difficult walks in the company of a guide. Low- and high-level walks can be booked with rangers from the Countryside Centre (01445 791368; Easter–September). You can also book a host of outdoor pursuits with Torridon Activities

(01445 791242; www.torridon-activities.com), including an excellent navigation course that equips you with the skills to find your way off the mountains in reduced visibility.

An alternative is to follow one of the area's classic lower-level trails to Coire Mhic Fhearchair. It takes around two hours to reach the coire from the A896 car park, but the ascent doesn't really get steep until you reach the waterfalls that signal your imminent arrival. The centrepiece of this stunning coire is the eponymous Loch Mhic Fhearchair, whose crystal-clear waters reflect the ancient sandstone hulk of the triple buttress that flanks its southern edge.

At the end of a strenuous day's walking amid some of Scotland's most impressive mountain scenery, you can, as you wash away any aches and pains in a free hot shower and settle down to a meal cooked on your campfire, celebrate your decision not to wild camp. If you can bear to take another short walk or an easy drive, dusk brings hordes of wild stags down to the roadside just to the north. The perfect end to your almost-wild-camping day.

THE UPSIDE You often have the deer and mountains all to yourself.
THE DOWNSIDE The site can get really boggy after heavy rain. It's also pretty small and can get busy in good weather.
THE DAMAGE There is no charge and bookings are not taken.
THE FACILITIES Toilets, hot showers and sinks with hot and cold water. The toilet block is located just outside the campsite and can be used by the general public too.
NEAREST DECENT PUB The Torridon Inn (01445 791242; formerly the Ben Damph Inn) lies 3 miles from the campsite (on the A896 towards Shieldaig) in a former stable block and has a welcoming bar and restaurant with upmarket pub grub (£10–12 for a main), a good selection of real ales and, of course, plenty of whiskies. The bar was once in the Guinness Book of Records for its malt selection. Now it has just 60 to choose from.
IF IT RAINS The only shelter other than your tent is the public toilet, so put on your waterproofs and prepare to brave the elements, but stick to low-level walks. Or chill out at the Torridon Inn (see above), which also has rooms.
GETTING THERE Heading north on the A9 from Inverness take the A835 towards Ullapool then the A832 towards Gairloch. After Kinlochewe turn left on to the A896 (signposted to Shieldaig) and look out for the right turn to Torridon. The campsite is on the right.
PUBLIC TRANSPORT There are bus services from Strathcarron to Torridon via Shieldaig, and from Lochcarron via Kishorn (see www.stagecoachbus.com for timetables).
OPEN All year.
IF IT'S FULL The Torridon Youth Hostel (08452 937373) charges £16.25 for a dormitory bed. You can also camp on common grazing land in Shieldaig (p199).

Torridon Campsite, Torridon, Achnasheen, Ross-shire IV22 2EZ

t | Info from Torridon Countryside Centre (01445 791368); Easter–Sept, 10am–5pm | 41 on the map

northern lights

If someone is prepared to wait over six years to secure the planning permission to build their new home, then you know that they must have found a very special spot indeed. Mike and Ethel Elliotts have been content to spend each summer tending their intimate campsite from the confines of a small touring caravan and, despite the absence of the finished self-build property that they so desperately want to live in, welcome you to Northern Lights as if it were the home they don't yet have.

In less time than it took to pitch our tent, we understood why the Elliotts were so dedicated to living in Badcaul. Set amid classic Highland scenery where the mountains and coast enjoy a dramatic dalliance, Northern Lights offers breath-halting views over Little Loch Broom, Badrallach and the hulk of Beinn Ghobhlach. If that is not enough, the light changes as frequently as the weather, bringing out a rich palette of greens, blues, purples and greys.

Even the most sceptical visitors succumb to Badcaul's charm, as Ethel, who is an expert storyteller, explained to us. It was with just the right measure of humour and pride that she recounted the tale of a Cheshire man who complained bitterly on arrival that the campsite was too small

(it has just 12 pitches), that there was nothing to do in this cast-adrift outpost of Scotland and, worst of all, he couldn't get any reception on his television. The soap addict curtly informed Ethel he was going to leave, but was overruled by his wife who had instantly fallen in love with Badcaul. Four days later he, too, had been won over by the ever-changing moods of the mountains and loch, or perhaps it had been the passing Minke whale he had run to tell Ethel about.

You've guessed it, despite missing a flurry of his essential soaps, our man from Cheshire ended up even more reluctant than his wife to leave after his epiphany. While it is not guaranteed that you will stumble upon a whale, you have a high chance of spotting porpoises frolicking in the loch below, red deer strolling by the site and some of the whole host of birds who call this ruggedly beautiful natural environment home.

If you are not content to simply relax and enjoy the views then there are plenty of opportunities to get about the place. Walkers from around the globe are drawn to Northern Lights campsite for the opportunity to tackle one of the better-known West Highland mountains, An Teallach. This imposing massif actually has three summits – Sail Lath (954 metres), Sgurr Fiona (1,060 metres)

and Bidein a Ghlas Thuill (1,062 metres) – so there are plenty of choices and challenges. A less strenuous alternative is to pick your way down to and around the rocky shores of Little Loch Broom.

Back at the site, Ethel and Mike have been working hard to upgrade the camping experience. They are currently renovating the toilet block, which is housed in a former croft, and now boasts new sink tops with a new tiled floor on the way. The rest of the simple campsite comprises a grassy field that slopes down towards the loch, with soft pitches opening up the views.

If, like the Elliotts, you fall in love with this remote corner of Ross-shire, maybe you will find yourself dreaming of the day that the Highlands and Islands Council grant you permission to build a home overlooking Little Loch Broom. Until then you will just have to make do, like the Elliotts, and enjoy it all from your temporary Highland home.

THE UPSIDE The views – see instantly why the Elliotts are so fond of this part of the world.
THE DOWNSIDE There is no telephone or email onsite, so if you want to book ahead you need to do it through the Larches Caravan Park in Cumbria, which is also owned by the Elliotts.
THE DAMAGE £5 for 1 person, £8 for 2 people and £2 per extra person. Dogs welcome too.
THE FACILITIES These are fairly rudimentary with toilets (2 for the ladies; 1 for the blokes, along with a couple of urinals), a metered hot shower in both the ladies' and the gents' (50p for 7 minutes) and washbasins; electric hook-ups, a rotary clothesline and a dishwashing area under cover.

NEAREST DECENT PUB Located 15 miles away on the shore of Loch Ewe, the Aultbea Hotel and Restaurant (01445 731201) boasts good views and lovely seafood such as dressed local crab and Loch Ewe scallops on a frequently changing, locally sourced menu. The Dundonnell Hotel (01854 633204) 4 miles away, is also a pretty safe bet for good food.
IF IT RAINS Put on your waterproofs to brave the elements and enjoy a bracing low-level walk.
GETTING THERE Heading north on the A9 from Inverness, take the A835 to Ullapool then the A832 towards Gairloch. After around 10 miles you will reach the campsite.

PUBLIC TRANSPORT The Westerbus (01445 712255) Gairloch–Inverness–Gairloch passes through Badcaul on Monday, Wednesday and Saturday. Timetables are available from www.rapsons.com/Timetable.html – Guide 5
OPEN Apr–end Aug.
IF IT'S FULL Wild camp around the shores of Little Loch Broom, taking care not to annoy the local landowners and following the advice laid out in the Wild Camping feature (see p160), or head around the loch to Badrallach campsite (p211).

Northern Lights Campsite, Croft 9, Badcaul, Dundonnell, Ross-shire IV23 2QY		
t	01697 371379 (Bookings via the Larches Caravan Park, Cumbria) or 07786 274175	
e	thelarches@hotmail.com	42 on the map

badrallach

You have to hand it to the Stott family. Not content with living in one of the most remote parts of the UK, in the Shetland Isles, they decided in 1991 to up sticks completely and create what has to be one of Britain's most remote campsites. They wasted no time converting three old crofts into a top little campsite with a bothy (a basic communal shelter in a remote location) on hand, so others could share in some of the most epic scenery in Britain.

The Stott family (Mick, Ali, Titus, Cosmo and Percy the dog) have created a wee gem on the site of the former crofts. The setting they chose is sublime, tucked right on the shores of Little Loch Broom (actually fairly grand as it sweeps past the site towards its climactic meeting with the Atlantic) with a chunk of huge Highland peaks vying for attention all around. Getting here is interesting too, as you have to negotiate a vertiginous single-track road that would tax a rally driver, but it is well worth the effort.

The site, which takes only 12 tents, consists of a grassy field where many people choose to camp in summer to avoid the worst of the midges – although they installed a 'midgebuster' in 2004, the little devils can still be troublesome. If you visit outside of midge season, or if you are just feeling plain daft and are doused in a liberal soaking of Avon Skin So Soft (the only thing we've found that ever seems to keep the little blighters at bay), then break away and choose one of the small private pitches set amid the heather. Here you can create your own hidden Highland idyll complete with a campfire. The beach beckons just a short way down a pebbly track and is as popular with campers as it is with sun-worshipping seals.

When the rains sweep in there is the bothy – a rudimentary shelter set up in an old barn that you can sleep in with a sleeping bag or just come and use for shelter or eating. Bothies are an integral part of Scottish outdoor culture and this is your chance to sample 'bothy life' without having to trek miles to get there. If you choose to stay here you can hire it exclusively; it's perfect for walkers as there is a peat stove you can cosy down around after a hard day in the hills.

The surrounding area is massively and deservedly popular with the walking community as there are countless peaks within easy reach, although you will need a car to get to the base of most. A Stott family favourite is An Teallach, a massive Munro that pokes over a kilometre high above the loch. Non-walkers can also hire out kayaks to paddle around the loch, rent bikes to explore the peninsula or try to master one of the power kites that take full advantage of the Atlantic winds. There is also bountiful salmon, sea trout and brown trout fishing on the brace of local estates.

It must have been hard to leave Shetland, but if you're going to move anywhere, then Badrallach is a pretty good choice. And in a moment of clarity – perhaps during a night spent around the campfire, with only the gentle lapping of Little Loch Broom and a shadow of Highland peaks for company – you will possibly find yourself agreeing with the Stott's romanticism that this is truly 'a timeless place'.

THE UPSIDE With this stunning scenery on the doorstep, you can see why the Stotts left Shetland behind to set up this intimate campsite.

THE DOWNSIDE Midges can be lethal in the heather; few wet-weather activity options for those without a car.

THE DAMAGE A wonderfully cheap £3 per adult and £1.50 for kids (2–16 years old) and £2.50 for a tent. The bothy is £5 per person per night.

THE FACILITIES Good facilities, with hot showers, a public telephone, electricity and decent toilets. There's also a shelter in the bothy if the elements are unkind.

NEAREST DECENT PUB The modern Dundonnell Hotel (01854 633204) is as close

as it gets, but it's still a slow drive back up the Badrallach road and then a mile or 2 further around the loch. The Broombeg Bar here awaits with pub grub, while classier fare is on offer in the Claymore Restaurant with a range including lamb, beef and venison dishes.

IF IT RAINS Either head to the bothy and cosy up by the peat fire to wait it out or head the 30 miles to Ullapool, where there's a great local bookshop, a fine chippy and several decent pubs (try the Ferry Boat Inn, 01854 612366, by the lochside).

GETTING THERE Take the A9 north from Inverness on to the A835 to Ullapool. Approximately 10 miles from Ullapool at Braemore Junction turn left on to the A832 for 10 miles then

turn right on to the single-track Badrallach road for approximately 7 miles.

PUBLIC TRANSPORT The Westerbus (01445 712255) Gairloch–Inverness–Gairloch passes the road end (7 miles from the site) on Monday, Wednesday and Saturday. For timetables see www.rapsons.com/pdf/guide_5.pdf. By prior arrangement, the owners can pick you up (for a small fee) from Ullapool, Garve or Inverness.

OPEN All year.

IF IT'S FULL Wild camp (see feature, p160) around the shores of Little Loch Broom, taking care not to annoy the local landowners, or skip around the loch to another *Cool Camping* favourite, the Northern Lights campsite (p205).

Badrallach, Croft 9, Badrallach, Dundonnell, Ross-shire IV23 2QP

| | t | 01854 633281 | w | www.badrallach.com | 43 on the map |

ardmair point

Alright, first things first. Ardmair Point is next to a road, it has over 100 pitches and a quintet of wooden chalets and caravans enjoy the best waterfront positions. But – and this is a big but – the site enjoys one of the most spectacular locations of any in Europe: set adrift on its own peninsula, with the Atlantic lapping at three sides, the Coigach Ridge rising impossibly steeply just to the north and the famed Summer Isles tempting on the horizon. Oh, and the fishing port of Ullapool, with its lively pubs and great food, is just three miles down the road.

Your attention will immediately be taken up by the views when you first arrive at Ardmair, as sea, hills and islands are all round. Once you've managed to tear your peepers away from these scenic treats and enter the site, you'll notice the efficient reception block that boasts a well-stocked shop selling everything from local maps and waterproofs through to kites and butteries – a strange east-coast 'delicacy'. If you are not lucky enough to have been force-fed them as a child and brainwashed into thinking you still have to eat them as an adult, imagine 100 croissants with a layer of lard laced between each, then squashed in an industrial vice, and you will have something approaching the artery-clogging

reality of butteries. Eat one and you won't need to eat again for weeks (trust us, we're speaking from experience).

The campsite offers a choice of areas to pitch on. There is the main grassy field, which has a gentle slope, but does not have any caravans. Most tenters head there, though watch where you pitch as there is some stony ground around. Arguably the best position is in the small clearing just below the site's highest point, though the midges tend to be in residence here when there is no breeze.

One of the most unusual aspects of Ardmair is that you can bring your own boat along on a trailer – or even arrive by boat if you like. Moorings are free, so you can sail up here and use it as a base or just launch your boat off the slipway and potter around the wide bay. Kayaks are also welcome with some top-notch paddling to be had around this rugged indented coastline, with its challenging Atlantic swells and unpredictable currents. And a good supply of wind provides all the pulling power needed for kite-surfers.

Land-based attractions include Ullapool Golf Club just down the road; not exactly championship quality but a fun course nonetheless. This being the Highlands there are numerous opportunities for walks, whether you are looking for a gentle stroll or a challenging adventure. Then, of course, there are the cruises out to the Summer Isles from Ullapool.

Ullapool itself is a major pull, a working port where real fishermen still drink real beer in real pubs. In this unpretentious little town, you can order a coffee in the tearoom and take it outside on to their 'terrace' – which happens to be the harbour wall, with impressive views of Loch Broom and the

brooding hills. The harbour wall also forms the beer garden of the best pub in town, the Ferry Boat Inn – well worth a visit.

Back at Ardmair, there can be a bit of traffic noise during the day and you'll certainly be aware of the caravans and chalets around, but by night as you savour a moonlit stroll along the pebble beach, any reservations about Ardmair soon disappear. Many visitors will die happy having experienced that viewscape. But beware: eat too many butteries and that might happen rather a lot sooner than you expect.

THE UPSIDE Stunning location with sea and hill views just a stone's throw from one of Scotland's most enjoyable fishing ports.
THE DOWNSIDE Caravans, tourers and the wooden chalets get the best views.
THE DAMAGE £11–17 for a tent, car and 2 people; £7 for a lone camper travelling on foot.
THE FACILITIES Modern facilities block (Scandinavian-style chalet) with washing machine, dryers, hot showers and hairdryers; electric hook-ups. There's also a kids' adventure playground to keep the nippers entertained onsite.
NEAREST DECENT PUB Ferry Boat Inn (01854

612366). Real ales, 'haggis, neeps and tatties', fresh local langoustines and Lochinver haddock feature regularly on the daily-changing menu in a pub where the craic flows as freely as the beer. Perhaps a bit too lively for some tastes at weekends, though.
IF IT RAINS Grab a slice of Highland culture as well as a slice of cake at Ceilidh Place (01854 612103; www.ceilidhplace.com). This multi-faceted café, restaurant, hotel, bookshop and ceilidh (informal gathering with live folk music and dancing) venue has been at the very heart of Ullapool life since 1970.

GETTING THERE From Inverness take the A835 towards Ullapool. The campsite is located on the left, 3 miles north of Ullapool.
PUBLIC TRANSPORT Take bus no. 961 from Inverness to Ullapool, then either the N67 or the 67A, which stop just outside the campsite. Call 08712 002233 for times.
OPEN Apr–Sept.
IF IT'S FULL Unless you fancy having a go at wild camping (see p160), it's a case of booking in advance or heading down to Badrallach (p211), which is a good 30 miles away.

Ardmair Point, Ardmair, Ullapool, Ross-shire IV26 2TN

| | t | 01854 612054 | w | www.ardmair.com | 44 | on the map |

shore

There cannot be many campsites in Britain as beautifully situated as Shore, and surely even fewer that come as such a shock to the system. The location, at the end of a series of very long cul-de-sacs (if that can make any sense) is stunning. Sutherland's mountains glower indignantly in the background, and the campsite itself winds through the dunes next to a tear-inducingly beautiful strand of dazzling white sand, lapped gently by the purest of clear turquoise waters.

By now you may be forming the impression that this is a vision of paradise, the perfect venue for a faraway romantic holiday, the kind of hideaway suited to whiling away quiet and contemplative hours absorbing the beauty of the surroundings. Well sorry, but no, it's a madhouse of sorts here. The *Cool Camping* research team, hoping for a get-away-from-it-all-in-the-middle-of-nowhere break, arrived during the school holidays and were surprised to find the campsite bursting at the seams, the scenic beach transformed into a scene of aquatic holiday mayhem. The sands were covered by a colourful selection of boating equipment ranging from speedboats and jet skis to sailing dinghies, canoes and all sorts of other equipment dedicated to zooming across the surf with a bouncing passenger

hanging off the seat. And aboard many of these aquatic vessels were giggling gaggles of happy campers from all over – Dundee, Glasgow, Manchester, Leeds, even Birmingham – laughing and splashing to their hearts' content.

They were all having the time of their lives and, what's more, everybody was sharing his or her nautical paraphernalia with everyone else. The youngsters who had brought canoes were lending them to the ones without, and all of them were seeing some action behind the jet skis and speedboats. Perhaps even more bizarre was the fact that the teenage hordes milling around the campsite were all exceedingly relaxed and very well behaved. And this, we gleaned after speaking to lots of regular campers here, wasn't just a one-off or temporary bit of hocus-pocus. Apparently, here at Shore good manners and quiet nights abound.

So, what looked initially like a scene from holiday hell – a paradise lost to a throng of ultra-enthusiastic water babies – was gradually turning into a very unique, and oddly idealistic, experience. The young campsite management and staff also do their bit to foster this sense of benign chaos in a beautiful place, arranging competitions

such as the Achmelvich Olympics, which involves all kinds of exhausting, fun events like good old welly-throwing, to get all the youngsters involved in the fun, no matter how reticent they may have been on arrival.

Of course, if you want to come here out of high season, when the impromptu Co-operative Holidays run by the campers aren't in operation, then Shore may well be a very different place, but that would be missing something really remarkable. In this world of risk assessment, health and safety, and general selfishness, it's a rare treat to see folk getting together and organising

their own fun without too much fear of making mistakes. And if you happen to have any teenagers, possibly lurking or sulking somewhere in the house, then this impromptu social gathering of a site could very well tempt them out and revolutionise their whole attitude to camping.

While we realise this site will not do for everyone – and there will definitely be those who won't appreciate the very idea of such a lively gathering in such a beautiful spot – it is exactly the polite mayhem running around this most picturesque of remote areas that makes it such a unique and alluring place.

THE UPSIDE Terrific fun for water sports fans, a great place for teens to give camping a whirl and it's in a stunning location to boot.
THE DOWNSIDE There's not much to do around here if you aren't a water sports fan; and if you're not keen on sharing your space with teenagers, avoid coming in peak season.
THE DAMAGE 1-person tent £6; 2-person £8; 3–4-person £9.50; 5–6-person £11; 7 or above £12.50. All plus £1 per adult; 50p per child. Electric hook-ups £3. No dogs allowed (not even assistance ones). No advance bookings taken.
THE FACILITIES Decent though not luxurious ablutions that include toilets, hot showers, laundry, and electric hook-ups. There is also a small shop

onsite, and this is vital as the nearest supermarket is 40 (yes forty) miles away.
NEAREST DECENT PUB There is nowhere within easy reach, so stock up and BYOB. Takeaway meals are available from the onsite chip shop during peak season.
IF IT RAINS The water sports carry on regardless of the weather, but there is nothing whatsoever to see or do in terms of tourist attractions nearby, and surely this is what helps make the atmosphere onsite so sociable.
GETTING THERE The quickest route is to head north beyond Inverness on the A9 then the A836 and A837 north and west, joining the A837 all the way to Lochinver, then follow signs to Achmelvich.

A more scenic option (if you have the time to spare) is to bumble north up the west coast from Kyle of Lochalsh.
PUBLIC TRANSPORT Bus no. 67A runs daily between Ullapool and Achmelvich via Lochinver (from Ullapool the journey takes about an hour). But we're not sure they allow canoes or speedboats on board, so if you're armed with any nautical equipment, best opt for the car.
OPEN Early Apr–end Sept.
IF IT'S FULL …or if you want somewhere less busy during the school holidays then Clachtoll Beach campsite (p225) is 4 miles further north along the lane.

Shore Caravan Site, 106 Achmelvich, Lochinver, By Lairg, Sutherland IV27 4JB

| t | 01571 844393 | w | www.shorecaravansite.yolasite.com | 45 on the map |

clachtoll beach

'Positively Mediterranean' is how one Drumbeg resident described a nice summer's day on the Assynt Peninsula. Admittedly it wasn't yet noon and the pint he was drinking in Lochinver's Caberfeidh pub probably wasn't his first. But at Clachtoll Beach campsite, owner Jim's tan is living proof that the Scottish climate can be kind.

Jim's a sunny kind of guy – chatty and genial and always eager to help out. He's not big on signs and instructions everywhere but he knows how he likes his campsite run and encourages folk to play by the rules just by using a little gentle persuasion. Not that you can't have fun. He once organised a bus to take a bunch of Edinburgh Uni students to the pub in Lochinver, brought them back and let them party on the beach till 4:30 in the morning, after which they were as good as their word and tiptoed back through the site so as not to wake anyone up.

Clachtoll's remote location and slightly tricky access (at one point on the 23-mile single-track road the maximum gradient is 25 per cent and it's known as 'the breakdown zone') doesn't dent its popularity. And come that Mediterranean summer the place can become a point of pilgrimage for anyone wanting to enjoy the seclusion.

The site's around 100 metres or so from the sea, set into the march grass behind the shallow dunes, and it can feel the full force of the wind when it whips up, so be warned: digging out Grandad's old army surplus tent from the garage might not be the best idea.

The beach isn't the kind of huge sweeping bay you'll find elsewhere, but a more intimate affair, sheltered by a fringe of black rocks and a high promontory on its left that does something to deflect the wind. Maybe that's why the sheep rather like it and are often to be found wandering the sands looking vacant.

This part of the north-west coast is heaven for walkers, with everything from easy coastal routes to wander, to some of Scotland's most remote and challenging peaks like Suilven and Stac Pollaidh (pronounced 'stack polly') within striking distance. There are even some woodland walks, which come as a pleasant surprise when so much of the area is completely treeless. One such wander takes you through the ancient Culag Woods by Lochinver, where birdlife such as herons and woodpeckers can be spotted going about their feathery business. Then there are all the watery things to do, from paddling in the surf

to boogie boarding and coasteering (one for the adrenaline junkies; it's a combination of rock climbing, scrambling and swimming around the coastline).

The Highland Clearances and natural migration to the New World did the job of winnowing out the population of these parts and it's never really recovered. But what remains are some marvellous little hamlets and human outposts in the vast green desert of the hills. Drumbeg's a fine example of a small thriving settlement, boasting an art gallery, a fine hotel and an award-winning little village shop with freshly baked bread,

fair trade and local organic produce. You can even order goods over the Internet. As they say, every little helps.

To the south is the main town of Lochinver, more a string of houses along the lochside than a town perhaps, but it does have the benefit of the Caberfeidh pub with its small riverside beer garden and a really good Tourist Information office if you're running short of ideas. Not that you should, though, with all that wilderness and water at your disposal. And what with the Mediterranean climate, there's no excuse for skulking in the pub. Particularly not before midday.

THE UPSIDE Chilled-out site on a coast boasting sandy coves, rocky hills and, occasionally, Mediterranean sunshine.
THE DOWNSIDE The beach and bay don't quite do justice to the location.
THE DAMAGE Tents are £8–12 depending on size plus £1.50 per adult and £1 per child (up to 16). Camper vans/caravans are £10. Water and electricity are £3 per night. Dogs are welcome as long as they're kept on leads.
THE FACILITIES Pretty faultless. There's a cosy block with a couple of showers and WCs (with nice wooden-framed prints in them), along with dishwashing facilities, a washing machine and

a tumble-dryer. There is also a public loo that's by the beach.
NEAREST DECENT PUB The Caberfeidh (01571 844321) in Lochinver is a decent boozer in the country line with a modest beer garden out back, next to the water.
IF IT RAINS According to Jim the most popular activity when it rains is to don a wetsuit, grab a boogie board and make for the surf.
GETTING THERE Clachtoll is on the B869 off the A837 just north of Lochinver. You can't miss the site on the left as you come down the hill. From the north, come off the A894 just past Kylesku, but it's a steep, twisty single-track road if

you come via Drumbeg. Maximum gradient is 25 per cent, so be warned.
PUBLIC TRANSPORT There's 1 postbus a day (the no. 123 operated by the Royal Mail), which runs from Lairg through Lochinver and past Clachtoll up to Drumbeg. Go to www.royalmail.com and type 'postbus' into the search box for details. It usually costs between £2 and £5 for a single journey.
OPEN Easter–end Sept.
IF IT'S FULL Either go wild or go north to the site at Scourie (p231) or south to Ardmair Point (p215).

Clachtoll Beach Campsite, 134 Clachtoll, Lochinver, Sutherland IV27 4JD

| t | 01571 855377 | w | www.clachtollbeachcampsite.co.uk | 46 | on the map |

scourie

Robert Burns, Scotland's great mythologiser of the mundane and the simple, wrote odes to such humdrum things as mice, lice and haggis. But he never eulogised the Scottish midge and with good reason. Midges are neither soft and furry nor very appetising. Besides, 'wee sleekit cow'rin'tim'rous *chironomidae*' doesn't scan very well.

Whereas many of Scotland's coastal campsites are too windy for midges, the sheltered bay at Scourie does, unfortunately, provide ideal flying conditions for the little blighters. However, that is no reason not to come and enjoy one of Sutherland's most tranquil sites. This region is one of the most sparsely populated in Europe and the scattered dwellings of the area's few human habitations seem to cling to the coast for safety.

Scourie is a tiny hamlet clustered around an inlet on the extreme north-west coast, 40 miles from Ullapool. The landscape here may be stark and sparse but the campsite is a little oasis of green. At first glance, you'd be forgiven for mistaking the green terraces for a nine-hole pitch-and-putt course, so immaculate is the grass. Caravans and motorhomes are largely confined to the areas around the amenities block, so tents have the run of the terraced pitches that extend down almost to the shores of the bay.

Scourie is an ideal stopping-off point between Ullapool and the far north coast around Durness, 25 miles from Scourie. From Durness, a coastal village that seems like something blown north from Cornwall by doomsday winds, a tiny boat takes you across the Kyle of Durness to rendezvous with a minibus that plies the only stretch of road in Britain not connected to any other road. It runs the 11 miles through an area called the Parph out to Cape Wrath, the most north-easterly point of the mainland and the site of a Stevenson lighthouse (worth a nose around). It's a favourite haunt of kite-surfers who can be seen from the cliff-tops clinging to their kites as the winds try to whisk them off to Spitzbergen.

For the intrepid there is a chillingly remote coastal walk from the crumbly chocolate cliffs of Cape Wrath back to the road from Kinlochbervie (see Walks and Wheel Trails, p88). The walk takes in the fantastic beach at Sandwood Bay and is so remote that it would make even Greta Garbo crave some company. The landscape here is not so much mountainous as pockmarked with massive towers of stone rising out of moorland.

Maybe that is why the Ministry of Defence uses much of the area as a bombing target. These distinct mountains must be easy for even the greenest trainee pilot to hit.

Heading south from Scourie towards Ullapool is the impressive Loch Assynt with the forlorn ruin of Ardvreck Castle sitting exposed to the whipping winds that sweep up the length of the loch. In 1650, the Marquis of Montrose, who had continued to fight for Charles I, even after the king's execution in 1649, was led from here, trussed and bound to a horse, to Edinburgh for execution. He was placed on his horse backwards and would have had a magnificent view of the receding castle as he was led away. Forty years later, the castle was ruined after a siege and left as it stands today, an empty but imposing shell.

After the sparseness of Sutherland, Ullapool feels like a metropolis. It's a small but bustling town and the main ferry route to the Outer Hebrides. Fresh fish is landed by a small fleet of brightly coloured trawlers, so it's no surprise that Ullapool also boasts the best chippy in Britain, at least according to the discerning listeners of Radio 4 back in 2004. It's known, appropriately enough, as the Chippy, a name whose simplicity Robert Burns would no doubt have admired.

THE UPSIDE Peace and tranquillity amid the far north-west coast's rugged beauty.
THE DOWNSIDE It can get busy in high season. And of course, there are those pesky wee sleekit cow'rin'tim'rous *chironomidae* to worry about.
THE DAMAGE Tent, car and 1 adult starts at £8.50; tent and cyclist is £6; 2 motorbikes, 1 tent and 2 adults is £10. Phone for further permutations. Dogs, less complicatedly, are free.
THE FACILITIES A clean toilet block with hot showers. Dishwashing and laundry also available. There is a small supermarket in Scourie.

NEAREST DECENT PUB The Anchorage pub onsite has a good atmosphere and serves up cracking food, while the Scourie Hotel (01971 502396), 2 minutes' walk away, serves real ale (with a changing selection of guest ales) and decent pub grub but in a rather fatigued setting.
IF IT RAINS Birds fly in the rain so take the boat to Handa Island (from Tarbert Pier) to watch the puffins, fulmers and shags.
GETTING THERE From Ullapool follow the A834 north to Ledmore Junction and turn left on to the A837. Along the shores of Loch Assynt, turn right up the hill on to the A894 and it's another 17 miles to go before you hit Scourie.
PUBLIC TRANSPORT Bus nos. N67 and S67 run north from Inverness via Ullapool and up the A838 to Scourie.
OPEN Mar–Sept.
IF IT'S FULL Head north to Durness where a dramatic campsite overlooks Sango Sands (p243) or south to Ardmair Point (p215), just north of Ullapool to camp by the shores of Loch Broom.

Scourie Caravan & Camping, Harbour Road, Scourie, Sutherland IV27 4TG

| t | 01971 502060 | 47 on the map |

Festivals and Events

There's more to Scotland than
the great outdoors, which, given
the weather, is just as well

Scotland's astonishing array of festivals and events reflects the country's eclectic past and optimistic view of the future. Whether you're into tartan, Travis or **Trainspotting**, there's a misty corner of the Scottish festival scene that'll suit you.

While much of Scotland's cultural life is to be found in the antagonistic twin cities of Edinburgh and Glasgow, the rest of the country is far from being just heather and grouse. There are some real gems as far afield as the Orkneys and Dumfries and Galloway.

Some of the best little festivals, fêtes and events are the ones you stumble upon by chance. But we thought we'd point out a few favourites to whet your appetite (whether that be for laughs, literature, music or muscley men hurling large objects as far as they can) and help send you on your way.

Edinburgh International Festival and Festival Fringe

This is the grandame of them all and the largest arts festival in the world. The main festival covers a vast spectrum of theatre, opera, dance and music, while the Festival Fringe is so broad that, quite, frankly it's beyond categorisation, but has a reputation for the strength of its comedy and an equal reputation for staging some stuff that's so rubbish you can only laugh. Along with the International Book Festival, the whole ensemble so dominates the city in August that the Film Festival has now moved to June to find a bit of space.

Edinburgh, Midlothian
www.eif.co.uk; August–September

Celtic Connections

First things first. This Glasgow music festival takes place in January, so it's a winter woollies and torch-lit-parade affair. As the name implies the music is of a traditional bent, some of it Celtic, some of it not – there's music to be heard from everywhere from Africa to Asturia. There's also an annual 'open stage' event where newcomers get the chance to shine. The whole thing seems like Glasgow's riposte to Edinburgh's gargantuan festival and holding it in January is quite clever because no one's going to be disappointed if the weather is bad.

Glasgow, Strathclyde
www.celticconnections.com; January–February

St Magnus Festival

Founded in 1977 by composer Sir Peter Maxwell Davies, this midsummer festival showcases Orkney at its best. It's fairly highbrow stuff, centring on orchestral and choral music and featuring courses on things like conducting and composing. But the Orkneys are so breathtaking and have such a vibrant artistic community that the festival almost becomes a celebration of the islands themselves. And there are venues to die for, such as the magnificent 12th-century St Magnus Cathedral in Kirkwall. Worth a visit, regardless of whether you're a fan of string quartets and plainsong or not.

Orkney Islands
www.stmagnusfestival.com; June

T in the Park

Scotland's multi-award-winning music festival takes place on a disused airfield, so it doesn't quite have the rural, Glastonbury feel. The 'T' is not the Miss Marple kind either but the initial of the brewing company that sponsors the event. This is Scotland after all. Still, 80,000 people can't all be wrong and the kind of headline acts that grace T in the Park year after year – think REM, the Killers and Radiohead – have cemented its place as one of the premier international music festivals. Such is the atmosphere at T, that many attendees pitch up and never leave the partying campsite.

The Old Air Field, Balado, Kinross-shire KY13 7NW
www.tinthepark.com; July

Highland Games

The advent of July means just one thing in northern Scotland: it's time to separate the men from the boys at the Highland Games. This competitive season sees numerous traditional events taking place across this heather-strewn land, from small-scale village fêtes to the sort of Braemar affair the Queen goes to in her regal wellies and favourite headscarf. The largest of them is the Cowal Highland Gathering at Dunoon, attracting over 3,000 competitors in everything from tossing the caber to the sword dance. But perhaps the best are those small local ones where Tavish puts his back out trying the sheaf toss and the 10-man band is so badly out of tune that everyone's forced into the pub.

www.visitscotland.com/guide/see-and-do/
eventshighlandgames; July–August

Beltane Fire Festival

This unique event takes place on the Beltane, one of the Celtic Quarter fire days. Well, more accurately, it lasts through the night of the 30th April and into the morning of the 1st May each year. Although it was only instigated in the 1980s, it draws its inspiration from that great well of May Day mythologies about fertility, the Green Man, the death of winter and the coming of summer. It's a riot of fire, body paint and dancing up on Calton Hill overlooking Edinburgh. Colourful dancers cavort through the night at various 'points' of earth, air, fire and water.

Calton Hill, Edinburgh, Midlothian
www.beltane.org; April (30th)–May (1st)

Glasgow International Comedy Festival

With the Edinburgh Festival Fringe becoming ever more comedy-dependent, here's Glasgow's take on having a laugh. Unfortunately, it's a bit early in the season for campers as it takes place in March, but this relative newcomer (it's been going less than a decade), spread across a number of venues all over the city, attracts some pretty funny names, from current hipsters like the irreverent Frankie Boyle to classy antiques like Joan Rivers and Dame Edna Everage. It also runs workshops and stuff for the kiddies and is allegedly the largest comedy festival in Europe. But then how big is Germany's?

Glasgow, Strathclyde;
www.glasgowcomedyfestival.com; March

The Wickerman Festival

Loosely inspired by the cult 1970s film *The Wicker Man*, this two-day festival takes place in late July in East Kirkcarswell in south-west Scotland. It's a mainline music festival with a line-up of indie/specialist guests, like Mercury nominees Sweet Billy Pilgrim. Pride of place, though, goes to the wicker man up on the hill, which is set ablaze at midnight on the Saturday, just like in the film (only without Edward Woodward simpering inside). Don't worry though – it's much more laid back and friendly than it sounds and is Scotland's latest up-and-coming festival.

East Kirkcarswell, Nr Dundrennan, Dumfries and Galloway DG6 4QW
www.thewickermanfestival.co.uk; July

sango sands

Sutherland is the least populated place in Britain; and while journeying north to reach the isolated community of Durness, the emptiness and desolation may prove slightly unnerving for city-slickers out on a rare trip north. For this reason, when the wide-eyed traveller finally rides into the wee village of Durness (population 400) it takes on the proportions and atmosphere of somewhere much, much bigger. It's surprisingly cosmopolitan, too, with visitors having struggled through the wilderness from seemingly every last corner on earth. And please, there is no need to point out that the earth has no corners, because the folk camping at Durness are definitely from them. There is even a sign at Sango Sands campsite that confirms where they are all from and just how far they've come to get here.

Travelling through the beautiful, brutal scenery to this top north-western corner of Scotland is a sensational experience, and taken slowly (stopping off at the other *Cool Camping* sites along the west coast, perhaps) this amazing journey will surprise, delight, shock, and provoke any other emotion it is possible to feel from wandering through such high, wild places. All have their wicked way with your soul, but Scotland saves the very best for the very last, when you reach Sutherland.

Once any sober mind has made it past Ullapool to Durness, it will be hard-pressed to recall any other place in Britain that quite captures this same essence of wilderness. Just rock and water line the route north for mile upon mile and white-tailed eagles watch your progress with beady eyes, waiting to pick over your bones, should misfortune befall you. To put this relentless emptiness into context, it's about the same distance from Ullapool to Durness as it is from Birmingham to Manchester, but there are less than a thousand people living on the land between. The scenery is absolutely awesome, and you never ever want the journey to end, but are almost relieved when civilisation finally comes into view.

This is the setting for Sango Sands. It wouldn't matter if this campsite doubled up as the local bus shelter, for it offers succour to the weary traveller when it seemed that the world had ended, which, in effect, it does just here. Sango Sands teeters on the northern edge of Britain in glorious fashion, a fitting end to the trek through all that emptiness – a view out to infinity.

If you can drag your eyes away from the view of mountains on two-and-a-half sides, and the endless ocean on the other three (really, this is fact, not an optical illusion) then the

campsite itself is fairly ordinary. But you can't and it isn't. There are caravans littering the site in places, but they are invisible because the scenery is that big. There are several toilet blocks, and we are sure they are absolutely fine, but despite several visits to Sango Sands our intrepid(ish) crew cannot remember a thing about them. All they can recall, collectively, is the astounding journey to get there, the mind-blowing view from the site and the delicious confectionery from the chocolate factory just down the road at the Balnakeil Craft Village.

Sango Sands is at the end of a very long road, through the most incredible scenery in the land, but don't think of this as a fitting finale, so much as a fantastic half-time break on the journey of a lifetime. That is, if you can bring yourself to head home again.

THE UPSIDE Amazing scenery and location, teetering on one of Britain's northernmost tips.
THE DOWNSIDE Can get a bit blustery (blowing tents clean away at times), and if you're from down south it's a long way home (1,000 miles to London) – don't go back, stay here.
THE DAMAGE Adults £5.75; first child £3.10, second child £1.50, additional children free (we hope the kids won't get a value complex). Electric hook-ups £3 each.
THE FACILITIES Modern and decent facilities including toilets, hot showers, laundry, and campers' kitchen – which includes a cooker.

NEAREST DECENT PUB There is a bar and restaurant (the Oasis) next to the site run by the campsite owners or, about a mile away, offering food and local music, lies the Smoo Cave Hotel (01971 511227; www.smoocavehotel.co.uk).
IF IT RAINS It will be travelling that fast you won't see it. The beach surrounding the site is great for surfing. Or head to Smoo Cave, it doesn't appear to leak too badly. Within walking distance are several cafés including the one at Cocoa Mountain (www.cocoamountain.co.uk), which is a small award-winning chocolate factory. A trip to Cape Wrath is another option that involves a ferry and minibus ride (01971 511343) or take your own bike if you don't mind getting wet.
GETTING THERE This is the far north-western edge of Scotland – every way here is beautiful, but the quickest is probably the A9 north beyond Inverness then the A836 and A838 to Durness.
PUBLIC TRANSPORT There's a regular, but infrequent, bus service from Inverness. See Traveline (www.travelinescotland.com) for times.
OPEN Generally Easter–mid Oct, or when the last campers leave.
IF IT'S FULL It's huge, it's a thousand miles from London, so, c'mon, it won't be full.

Sango Sands Caravan and Camping, Sango Sands, Durness, Sutherland IV27 4PP

| t | 01971 511262 | 48 on the map |

dunnet bay

When you take it at face value, this site should be everything that *Cool Camping* is not: a council-owned site; run by the Caravan Club, with wardens in mint-green uniforms; and rules everywhere.

Now it's true that at the height of summer it can seem like Caravan City with room for only a few tents jammed up against the dunes. But therein lies the secret. The site is slap-bang next to the sand dunes of a huge sweeping bay. Long stalks of dune grass practically reach over a small wooden fence to touch your tent.

The restless waves of the Pentland Firth attract surfers from far and wide. But Dunnet Bay is one of the north coast's trump cards. With a mile or more of white sand stretching like a crescent moon to the cliffs of Dunnet Head, the most northerly point of mainland Britain, it's a spectacular setting. With a bit of sunshine, a few tinnies of beer and the odd shout of 'Ripper, mate!' and you could swear you were on Bondi Beach in Australia. Well, almost.

For those with a head for heights, there's a road roaming for five miles over bleak and brown scrubland up towards the cliff-top at Dunnet Head. Up there is the lighthouse built by Robert Louis Stevenson's grandfather with views over Gills Bay and across the channel between the headland and Scapa Flow in the Orkneys. On a clear day, you can see the breadth of Scotland from up here – from Cape Wrath in the east to John o'Groats in the west – and it's worth putting up with a few too many caravans at the campsite for that alone.

THE UPSIDE Beautiful sandy bay and grassy dunes among which to pitch your tent.
THE DOWNSIDE The site is mainly for caravans and has relatively few pitches for tents.
THE DAMAGE Varies with the season. High season is £7 per person plus £2 for a small tent or £4 for a large. Dogs are allowed but must be kept on a lead.
THE FACILITIES Pristinely kept toilets and hot showers. Dishwashing and laundry facilities are also available. BBQs are allowed onsite but open fires are banned.
NEAREST DECENT PUB The lounge bar at the Northern Sands Hotel (01651 842214; www.northernsands.co.uk), half a mile away, has leather chairs and wood panelling and serves a decent pint and excellent sandwiches. For those who want a little more rock with their roll, head over to Thurso for Top Joe's at the Central Hotel (01847 893129).
IF IT RAINS Visit Mary-Ann's cottage in Dunnet village. It's an old croft, left intact after the death of its 93-year-old owner – and she had kept it just as her grandfather had.
GETTING THERE Follow the A836 for 7 miles from Thurso to the sands of Dunnet Bay. The site is between the road and the dunes.
PUBLIC TRANSPORT A regular daily bus service runs from Thurso to Dunnet (except on Sundays).
OPEN Generally early Apr–early Oct, but the dates change slightly each season, so if it's spring or autumn best check before you go.
IF IT'S FULL There is a campsite in Thurso (01847 895782) if required, but for a little extra cash there are 9 rooms at the cosy and comfortable Northern Sands Hotel (see Nearest Decent Pub), ranging from £35 per night single to £70 per night double.

Dunnet Bay Caravan and Camping Site, Dunnet, Thurso, Caithness KW14 8XD

| | t | 01847 821319 | w | www.caravanclub.co.uk | 49 | on the map |

wheems organic farm

Not for nothing did the poet and novelist George Mackay Brown say that the Orkney imagination was haunted by time. There's something other-worldly about the Orkney Islands. There's been a human presence here for thousands and thousands of years; the living in places like Skara Brae and the dead in the Neolithic burial chamber of Maes Howe, whose entry shaft is perfectly aligned with the setting sun on the winter solstice. It's like the place knows things you don't, things buried so deep you'd spend a lifetime trying to find them. Which is, of course, what many people choose to do here – the islands' population is around 20,000.

The land's been smoothed over by the year-round westerly winds and the resulting views are of rolling hills and water, water everywhere between the 70 islands that make up the archipelago. The dun-coloured hills are like the patternless tweed of a geography teacher's jacket and the sky can do everything from broody to menthol clear.

Many visitors arrive on the short ferry hop from Gills Bay, between Thurso and John o'Groats, to the charming little port village of St Margaret's Hope. From there it's a couple of miles over the hill to Wheems Organic Farm, owned and run by Christina, a former oboist with the Scottish Chamber Orchestra, and Mike, a landscape architect. Their outlook on life, the universe and camping is to keep things small, share in the beauty of the place and pass on the philosophy of eco-living.

Wheems is such a great name it should really be a brand, like Ben & Jerry's ice cream or Innocent smoothies. But the farm produces only organic eggs and veg, neither of which lend themselves to advertising chic. If eggs, for example, could be branded, the Americans would have already done it by now and we'd all be slicing the tops off our Ee-Z-Eggs for breakfast. Besides, it would all seem out of place in Orkney.

There's an abundance of good food too, and if you stay at Wheems you're only an organic egg's throw from one of Scotland's best restaurants, the Creel (01856 831311), in St Margaret's Hope. It's a great example of a local restaurant doing local things with local products and is well worth a visit; though it's advisable to book ahead. Alternatively, there's a wealth of local produce back at Wheems so you'll have no excuse not to rustle up something yourself.

Like all things in the farming line there's no pretence here that Wheems falls into the 'lap of luxury' camping category. But what

it lacks in creature comforts it more than makes up for (in droves) with its hospitality, location and coastal views.

St Margaret's Hope is a charming little port village where the Gills Bay ferry docks. Since the Second World War the islands of South Ronaldsay and St Mary's have been linked to the mainland by the Churchill Barriers, giant causeways built by Italian POWs. Admittedly they were primarily anti-submarine defences but now they mean that Kirkwall's only a 20-minute drive away.

Kirkwall seems a bit disappointing at first, particularly when you learn that it's an old Viking town dating back to the 11th century. But take a wander around its labyrinth of stone-paved streets past the magnificent cathedral of St Magnus and you'll soon be lost in all its misty history.

On your way back south, it's worth stopping at the small Italian chapel on Lamb Holm, built by and for the POWs while they were here and skillfully preserved. Like most things in the Orkneys, it's simple and unassuming but beautifully done.

THE UPSIDE Philosophically spot-on organic eco-camping with a warm welcome.
THE DOWNSIDE The camping field's on a slope.
THE DAMAGE It starts from £5 for a tent plus 1 person, and goes up according to tent size and number of people. Each additional person (over 3 years of age) is £3 and a car is £1. Campers and caravans start from £6 with 1 person (no hook-ups though). Dogs are accepted (under control) and are not charged for their stay.
THE FACILITIES There are 2 showers and 3 WCs in a wooden building by the bothy. There's also a sink for dishwashing (and a kettle) in the draughty outer area.
NEAREST DECENT PUB There are 3 in St Margaret's Hope. Don't bother with the Belle Vue

and pick either the Murray Arms (01856 831205; the livelier) or the Galley Inn (01856 831526), which is the smaller.
IF IT RAINS Make a pilgrimage to the tiny chapel, built by Italian POWs held here during the Second World War. They also built the causeways that link South Ronaldsay with the 'mainland'. The interior of the chapel is as striking as something you'd find in Rome.
GETTING THERE Easiest route from the mainland is the passenger ferry from John o'Groats or the car ferry from Gills Bay, both of which go to St Margaret's Hope. Follow the road from the ferry up through the village to the top of the hill and the main road to Kirkwall. Turn right then left (at the soldier's statue). Follow this road for a

mile or so until the crossroads (where there's a postbox). Go straight over and the farm is down the hill on the left.
PUBLIC TRANSPORT There's a reasonably frequent bus service in the summer months from Kirkwall to St Margaret's Hope (plus there's the ferry) but then it's a 2-mile walk from the town.
OPEN Early Apr–end Oct.
IF IT'S FULL It never has been. There's a second field that can take any overflow or there's a backpackers' hostel, St Margaret's Cottage (01856 831637) in St Margaret's Hope. Otherwise in Kirkwall there's the (fairly bog-standard) Pickaquoy Centre site (01856 879900).

Wheems Organic Farm, Wheems, Eastside, South Ronaldsay, Orkney KW17 2TJ

| | t | 01856 831556 | w | www.wheemsorganic.co.uk | 50 | on the map |

acknowledgements

Cool Camping: Scotland (2nd edition)
Series Concept and Series Editor: Jonathan Knight
Researched, written and photographed by:
Keith Didcock, Andy Stothert, Robin McKelvie
and Jenny McKelvie
Editor and Project Manager: Sophie Dawson
Design: Roz Keane
Cover Design: Kenny Grant
Proofreaders: Nikki Sims, Leanne Bryan
Publishing Assistant: Cassidie Alder
Marketing: Shelley Bowdler
PR: Carol Farley

Published by: Punk Publishing, 3 The Yard,
Pegasus Place, London SE11 5SD

Distributed by: Portfolio Books, 2nd Floor,
Westminster House, Kew Road, Richmond,
Surrey TW9 2ND

All photographs © Keith Didcock/Andy Stothert/Robin
McKelvie/Jenny McKelvie, except the following (all
reproduced with permission; t = top, b = bottom, r =
right, l = left): 4 tr & 11 br © David Dean/Lazy Duck;
89 bl © P Tomkins/VisitScotland/Scottish Viewpoint
(www.visitscotland.com); 90 bl © D Chadwick/
istockphoto; 91 bl © P Tomkins/VisitScotland/Scottish
Viewpoint; 130 b © David Dean/Lazy Duck; 210 tr,
b © Michael Stott/Badrallach 236 © P Sandground/
Edinburgh International Festival (www.eif.co.uk);
238 tr © Edinburgh International Festival (www.eif.
co.uk), bl © Lieve Boussauw/Celtic Connections; 239
tr © Clive Barda/St Magnus Festival; bl © T in the
Park 2009; 240 tr © P Tomkins/VisitScotland/Scottish
Viewpoint, bl © Anne Leven/istockphoto; 241 tr ©
Magners Glasgow International Comedy Festival, bl ©
Patrick and June Rafferty/Wickerman Festival.

Front cover: Sango Sands © Andy Stothert.

Many of the photographs featured in this book are
available for licensing. For more information, see
www.coolcamping.co.uk.

The publishers and authors have done their best
to ensure the accuracy of all information in *Cool
Camping: Scotland*, however, they can accept no
responsibility for any injury, loss or inconvenience
sustained by anyone as a result of information
contained in this book.

Punk Publishing takes its environmental
responsibilities seriously. This book has been
printed on paper made from renewable sources and
we continue to work with our printers to reduce our
overall environmental impact. Wherever possible,
we recycle, eat organic food and always turn the
tap off when brushing our teeth.

A BIG THANK YOU! Thanks to everyone who has
written and emailed with feedback, comments and
suggestions. It's good to see so many people at one
with the *Cool Camping* ethos. In particular, thanks
to the following readers for telling us about their
favourite places to camp: Jan Broderick, Hazel Dunn,
Claire Garrett, James Hepher, Rosemary Jackson and
Laura Russell.

HAPPY CAMPERS?

We hope you've enjoyed reading *Cool Camping:
Scotland* and that it's inspired you to get out there.

The campsites featured in this book are a personal
selection chosen by the *Cool Camping* team.
None of the campsites has paid a fee for inclusion,
nor was one requested, so you can be sure of an
objective choice of sites and honest descriptions.
We have visited hundreds of campsites across
Scotland to find this selection, and we hope you
like them as much as we do. However, it hasn't
been possible to visit every single Scottish
campsite. So, if you know of a special place that
you think should be included, we'd like to hear
about it. Send an email telling us the name and
location of the site, some contact details and why
it's special. We'll credit all useful contributions in
the next edition of the book, and senders of the
best emails will receive a complimentary copy.
Thanks and see you out there!

scotland@coolcamping.co.uk